O'BRIEN, George Dennis. Hegel on reason and history; a contemporary interpretation. Chicago, 1975. 188p 74-7560. 8.50. ISBN 0-226-61646-0

CHOICE　　*OCT. '75*

Philosophy

Like B. T. Wilkins (*Hegel's philosophy of history,* CHOICE, Jul.-Aug. 1974) O'Brien shows how Hegel's text speaks to the problem of historical explanation in contemporary critical philosophy of history. However, in spite of some overlap, O'Brien also deals with other aspects of Hegel's position and composes an interesting and different contemporary interpretation that complements the work of Wilkins. O'Brien contends that Hegel's four subcategories of reflective history constitute a dialectical development leading to philosophical world history — a reflection on the human struggle for social self-consciousness and freedom as it developed in the peoples, the individuals of history. Hegel's concept of reason in history is taken as an overcoming of the dichotomy between speculative and critical philosophy of history and also between subjectivity and objectivity in history. O'Brien recovers the original outline of the work in Hegel's appropriation of Aristotle's four causes — reason is made the end (freedom), the matter (states), the means (passion), and the form (the constitutions) of history. Reason as the principle for the construction and comprehension of the historical reality seems to make the historical consciousness deeper and more profound than has been thought.

Hegel on Reason and History

A Contemporary Interpretation

George Dennis O'Brien

The University of Chicago Press

Chicago and London

George Dennis O'Brien is dean of the college
and professor of philosophy at Middlebury
College.

The University of Chicago Press, Chicago 60637
The University of Chicago Press, Ltd., London

International Standard Book Number: 0-226-61646-0
Library of Congress Catalog Card Number: 74-7560

To
George Francis O'Brien
and
Helen Fehlandt O'Brien

Contents

Acknowledgments

I wish to express my gratitude to Middlebury College for financial support and for granting me an administrative leave during the academic year 1971-72 from my responsibilities as dean of the college. I also wish to thank the American Council of Learned Societies for a fellowship which made it financially possible for me to spend the entire period pursuing the research necessary for completing this book. To my Middlebury College colleagues Stanley Bates and Pardon Tillinghast, who waded through the text and offered encouragement and criticism, I offer compassion and gratitude. There can be few gestures more friendly than reading a person's commentary on Hegel. Finally, felicity to my wife, who not only suffered with serenity through months of protestations that philosophy is too difficult for mortal men, but who, during that time, probably made a more profound comment on the meaning of history, by bearing a child, than either Hegel or I could manage.

1 *Introduction*

The most readily available and probably the most widely read Hegel text in English translation is a small volume entitled *Reason in History*.[1] Not only is it used in courses in the philosophy of history, it is often used as a general introduction to Hegel's entire system in survey courses on the history of philosophy. The reasons for the choice are easy to discover. Unlike the *Phenomenology* or the *Logic*, it is a relatively simple text without the complex technical jargon of those major works. Moreover, Hegel's philosophy of *history* is something which even the common reader can more or less understand (even though he is likely to find it highly implausible), and it is well known that Hegel's views on historical development have been politically very potent in their Marxist version. This widespread use of *Reason in History* as a prime Hegel text for English readers, while perfectly understandable, is not without paradox, however.

Surely the most paradoxical aspect of its broad use is the dubious nature of the text itself. I will discuss the textual problems below, but it suffices to mention that Hegel actually never wrote a work entitled *Die Vernunft in der Geschichte* [*Reason in History*]; that large portions of the text are not from Hegel's manuscripts; and that the translation available—although it is a good translation—is not from the preferred German edition. Despite the shakiness of the text, the choice of this work for nonprofessionals remains valid. Even in older and less accurate translations like Sibree's,[2] from older and less accurate German editions, the general lines of Hegelian historical interpretation are clear. As Carl Friedrich says about Sibree while noting the variant editions: "The subtle points of divergence, interesting to the specialist, may well be neglected by him who wishes to get the vision that was Hegel's."[3] And it is Hegel's philosophy of history which fascinates the general reader, who would be utterly lost in the intricacies of his theory of the syllogism.

The nonprofessional may not only have a personal interest in getting at "the meaning of history" but he may feel a positive duty to comprehend the roots of Marxism so that he can understand the political events of the last one hundred years.

If the widespread use of the text seems paradoxical, given its provenance, there is perhaps a more profound curiosity in the fact that this work is widely read at all by professional philosophers working in English. At the risk of indulging in a historical generalization even broader than those found in Hegel, it is roughly correct to note that most professional philosophers writing in English have almost no sympathy for Hegel in general or for his philosophy of history in particular. The dominant school of philosophy in Great Britain and the United States has received a variety of descriptions: ordinary language, analytic, positivist, linguistic analysis; and there are sharp quarrels about methods and principles within the general field of "analytic" philosophy. Nevertheless, almost without exception, these philosophers reject Hegel as metaphysical, speculative, antiempirical, a priorist, hyperbolic, and, frequently, politically dangerous. There has been a broad suspicion that Hegel is not only wrong on this or that point, but that his whole conception of how to philosophize is profoundly mistaken and empty of fruitful results. Given the natural change in philosophic fashions, one suspects that Hegel might easily have passed into the limbo of unread greats, along with Malebranche, Fichte, Schopenhauer, and Whitehead, but for his work in the philosophy of history. Although analytic philosophy maintains a certain scholastic insularity to the headier issues of the day, even dons and professors can hardly ignore the immense impact of dialectical history on political thought. Moreover, in the years following the Second World War, a modest revival of philosophy of history in the "analytic" mode occurred which favored a continued reading of Hegel. Analytic philosophers of history in explaining the origins of their study noted that there was another kind of philosophy of history, "speculative" philosophy of history, exemplified by Hegel, from which their own work should be distinguished. Given this dichotomy of types of philosophy of history (which I discuss at some length in chapter 2), Hegel has retained a place in the curriculum as a kind of bogie to be avoided at all costs. In short, *Reason in History* continues to be read in English-speaking philosophy classes partly because of the profound lack of sympathy with its entire philosophical project. It is difficult to think of another philosophical work currently in circulation which plays a similar role.

A final peculiarity to be noted is that, despite the wide political influence of Hegel's views about historical development and the relatively broad readership of his work on the philosophy of history, no commentary of any extent has been published dealing directly with his text on history. There is a brief treatment by Jean Hyppolite of Hegel's philosophy of history which has not been translated into English and which is concerned with the general interest in history displayed by Hegel throughout his career rather than with the particular text of his lectures on the philosophy of history.[4] Many writers have emphasized the central importance of historical thinking in Hegel, but strangely enough, no one has so far applied the general lessons of Hegelian philosophy to the text of *Reason in History*. With this constellation of circumstances—wide readership, political importance, and lack of scholarly commentary—it seemed to me that my efforts at elucidation, imperfect as they may be, would serve some purpose. I do not agree with the negative assessment of Hegel's view on history which is so widespread, but I do agree with the equally widespread conviction that Hegel would rank near the bottom of any list of philosophical communicators. I have attempted to make clear what I believe to be Hegel's message and its value. In so doing, I have tried to keep in mind a potential audience of "analytic" philosophers as well as interested historians and the common reader. Thus, while my own interpretation has been profoundly influenced by French commentators like Kojève, I have attempted throughout to avoid elucidating Hegelian technicalities through existentialist or Marxist technicalities. With that general intention stated, let me turn to the general strategies of the commentary.

The Text: Reason in History

Before proceeding to discuss the philosophical strategy of this study, it is necessary for me to be clear about what work of Hegel's is under investigation. The work I shall be treating is the text entitled *Die Vernunft in der Geschichte* edited by Johannes Hoffmeister and published in 1955.[5] This text is referred to on its title page as "Fünfte, abermals verbesserte Auflage," and it has not yet been translated into English. It corresponds *roughly*, however, to the small volume *Reason in History* translated by R. S. Hartman, noted above. In essence what we are dealing with is the introduction to the *Lectures on the Philosophy of History*, that is, the general outline of the problems of a philosophy of history, rather than Hegel's extended commentaries on various cultures and historical periods which make up the bulk of that text. Hoffmeister's edition is the *fifth* edition in a series initiated by Georg Lasson in 1917, but in terms of all editions it is actually the *eighth* edition. A first edition was prepared by Hegel's pupil Eduard Gans in 1837, and there were two further editions by the philosopher's son, Karl Hegel. The principal English translations are the Sibree translation of *Vorlesungen über die Philosophie der Geschichte*[6] (from an edition of Karl Hegel's) and Hartman's more modern translation of the introductory sections from the same German edition. Hoffmeister's last German edition is certainly a preferred text, and I have with a few minor exceptions based my argument on the material and arrangement of that text. Nevertheless, the general character of the argument is reasonably clear even in the English translations from the older Karl Hegel texts, and I have followed the practice of citing both Hoffmeister and Hartman. I have followed Hartman wherever possible in translation. When I refer to *Reason in History*, I am referring to the Hoffmeister edition and to the parts of the *Vorlesungen* which roughly correspond to it and which constitute only the general introduction of the longer text. When, on occasion, I refer to *The Philosophy of History*, it is to the Karl Hegel/Sibree version.

A history of the German editions does not sufficiently characterize the work being studied. Basically, what we are dealing with in the Hoffmeister edition is the best possible reconstruction of Hegel's lectures. The reconstruction is based on a manuscript in Hegel's own hand, the notes taken of the lectures by three students, and earlier editions of Gans and Karl Hegel.[7] *Die Vernunft in der Geschichte*, then, is not, as such, a book of Hegel's. Hoffmeister's edition clearly separates the manuscript material from the *Nachschriften* by setting the manuscript material in cursive type. This assemblage of texts reconstructing Hegel's lectures makes the work of a commentator particularly difficult. A purist could simply ignore everything except the autograph manuscript, but no editor has so far thought fit to do so. The use of the lecture notes seems a reasonable gesture to fill in the incompleteness of the manuscript. The auditors may have been inaccurate on occasion, but they presumably did not construct the material out of whole cloth. It seems eminently sensible to believe that Hegel did cover the various topics set forth in their notes and in something like the order indicated in Hoffmeister's text. For this reason I have not scrupled overly in noting when material is manuscript and when it is *Nachschriften*. This procedure is in keeping with that of most scholars commenting on the considerable range of "Hegel" material put together in similar fashion, for example, his lectures on art and religion. Carl J. Friederich's attitude seems to be typical and eminently sensible:

> Hegel's *Philosophy of History* consists of lecture notes collated
> and edited after his death; only the main part of the introduction
> [the text entitled *Die Vernunft in der Geschichte*] has been pub-
> lished, by modern scholars, in accordance with Hegel's own man-
> uscript.... There has been a good deal of learned discussion as
> to how far one might go in accepting these lectures as authentic.
> There can be little question that the works written and published
> by Hegel himself like the *Phenomenology*...have a superior claim
> when one comes to controversial points. At the same time, one
> sympathizes with Kuno Fischer, when he insists that the philos-
> opher owes a great and permanent gratutide to the devoted labors
> of these pupils of Hegel who compared different sets of notes
> and tried to present a generally faithful portrait of these lectures.[8]

I emphasize, then, the somewhat tenuous character of the work at hand. Even the title, *Reason in History*, is an editorial invention but surely one amply justified by the central doctrine of the text. Since one strategy of my work is to lay out an ordered argument in the text, someone aware of the way in which *Die Vernunft in der Geschichte* came to be might consider the whole project bizarre. How can one claim that there is a connected and developing series of reflections in a text pasted together by a century and a half of editors? In chapter 2, for instance, I argue that there is a dialectical progression of methods of history from "original history" through "reflective history" to "philosophical history." Unhappily, the last three species of historical methodology are mentioned in the *Nach-schriften*, not in the Hegel manuscript. Shall we assume, then, that Hegel's account of methods broke off with "pragmatic history"? Did the auditors create these other species of historical meth-odology? It is highly implausible. I assume that Hegel did expand in his actual lectures along the lines indicated and in the order indicated. My only complaint against the auditors is that they did not take more notes, since one must often guess from their cryptic accounts how Hegel actually developed the argument.

Philosophical Strategies

This is a long book on a short "nonbook." At times it may appear to make things more difficult than they need be. Although *Reason in History* is widely taught because it is "easy," the very acceptance of it as a simple work can lead to serious misreadings. Because it is less jargon-filled and technical than the *Logic* or the *Phenomenology*, one can easily believe that he grasps the philosopher's point. I judge that underlying these lectures on history, however, there are the basic subtleties of Hegel's central philosophical notions and that, if these subtleties are not drawn out, the work will be badly misunderstood.

The basic problems of Hegel's thoughts on the philosophy of history finally do not, in my judgment, turn on nuances of translation or textual rearrangement. Even Sibree's rather old-fashioned translation states the fundamental lines of Hegel's views on the centrality of reason in history. The basic problem is philosophical. Just what is one to make of the great claim at the beginning of the 1830 lectures that reason is power, substance, content, and the end of history? No translation can make that claim easy to comprehend. (This passage is from Hegel's autograph manuscript, and since it is *the* passage about which my entire commentary turns, I can at least have that much assurance that I am writing about Hegel rather than Griesheim, Kehler or Stieve—the student auditors.)

This commentary is intended to be a philosophical rather than a philological commentary on the text. I have derived my philosophical direction from two considerations, one internal to Hegel, the other external. Internally, I have continuously assumed that *Reason in History* rests on foundations which are discussed at great length and with much intricacy in his major philosophical works such as the *Phenomenology*. For example, in discussing the lectures of 1822 and 1828, outlining a series of "methods" for writing history, I have assumed that buried beneath that sketchy and fragmentary text there is a dialectical progression similar to the dialectical progressions that occur throughout the major texts. By assuming that Hegel has a dialectical progression of methods in mind, one is able

to put an order into the argument that is not immediately evident
and that, I believe, illuminates the nature of the task set forth by
Hegel for "philosophy of history."

In addition to methodological assumptions about Hegel's philosophy, I have also attempted to indicate how the central claims of
Reason in History rest on notions which have been carefully
delineated in other works. Nothing contributes as much to the
misconceptions of Hegel's philosophy of history as a failure to
understand the special and "technical" sense in which he uses such
central notions as reason. At least when the reader comes across
some fuzzy notion like "spirit" he is forewarned that he may not
understand what is being said, but it is easy to assume that terms
like "reason" or "passion" or "nature" are simple enough when, in
fact, they have subtle nuances of meaning for Hegel which, if not
appreciated, may reduce his arguments to nonsense. Thus, one of
the most famous statements in *Reason in History* is Hegel's claim
that nothing great in history can occur without "passion." This is
frequently cited and it has a nice rhetorical ring to it. It should be
obvious, however, that the statement can hardly be accepted at face
value if his views are to have even the slightest internal consistency.
Just how does one reconcile that pungent claim with the dominant
thesis that reason is the sole force in history? The casual reader and
the careful philosopher may easily regard passion and reason as
competing claimants to the motive force in human action; if this is
so, Hegel's theory seems hopelessly confused. The very fact that
Reason in History has a readability quotient several times higher
than most Hegelian works is often a factor in its misunderstanding.
There has been a tendency for commentators to extract striking
epithets and set them up as epitomes of Hegel's views without
realizing how carefully they must be integrated into the entire
scheme of Hegelian notions. Again a famous example: many people
know of Hegel's claim that the only lesson we learn from history is
that people do not learn from history. That is a nice paradox,
memorable and expressing a kind of cynical wisdom that may
impress. Such an interpretation, however, is in my judgment a very
serious misreading of Hegel's point. It is not that the lessons are
there but we are too sluggardly to apply them. The message is much
more radical: there are no *lessons* of history in a conventional sense,
and that is what makes the use of history for pointing political or
moral examples so useless.

The primary source for the developed principles which I use to illuminate the obscure parts of *Reason in History* and philosophically deepen its rhetorical phrases is *The Phenomenology of Mind.*[9] Although there has been something of a split in twentieth-century Hegelian scholarship between those who emphasize the system of the *Encyclopedia* and those existentialist interpreters who prefer the explorative style of the *Phenomenology*, I share the opinion of Hyppolite that the divergence is exaggerated. Hegel appears to me remarkably consistent throughout his life in the major vision he has of the life of spirit. The *Phenomenology* happens to be the work of Hegel (other than *The Philosophy of History*) with which I am most conversant, and, besides, it has been subject to at least two superb commentaries (Jean Hyppolite's and Alexandre Kojève's) which in their differing ways emphasize the unusual importance of historical thinking in Hegel's overall philosophical position.[10] Kojève's work, now partially translated into English, offers an unusually powerful and persuasive account of the intricate arguments of the *Phenomenology*. My own views on Hegel are deeply influenced by Kojève, as will become obvious to anyone reading this commentary who is familiar with his work. Kojève is particularly insistent on the unique character of historical reality and on Hegel's unique position as the philosopher of that mode of reality. This is the central thesis of my commentary also. My work differs from Kojève's in two important respects, however. In the first place it is addressed to Hegel's lectures directly concerned with the philosophy of history rather than to the *Phenomenology*, which is Kojève's exclusive interest. Second, Kojève is writing out of the continental European philosophical position which has been heavily influenced by Marxist and existentialist themes. As a work of elucidation, therefore, it will not always serve for English-speaking audiences more influenced by "analytic" philosophy. Neither technical Marxism nor existentialism enjoy much more favor in American and British philosophy departments than Hegel himself, so that a commentary addressed to an audience conversant with Lukacs or Sartre may fail to serve for students of Hempel or Ryle. Commentaries are, after all, rhetorical exercises in which the nature and level of understanding in the audience is a guiding principle. My hope is to translate the insights of Hegel (and of Kojève) into terms more current in English philosophical work.

Any commentary must involve some rewriting or reconstruction of the text under study (if the original was pellucid, commentary would be otiose). In the case of Hegel the amount of reconstruction may be extensive. Kojève, for instance, generates pages of detailed exposition over a single line in the *Phenomenology*, and often one has the feeling that Hegel really should have graced us with the details of the argument which Kojève is forced to supply. In the case of *Reason in History* the temptation to reconstruct the argument is even more strong because of the imperfect state of the text. This is a temptation which I have not always sought to overcome. There is another aspect of "reconstruction" that should be pointed out, however, and this relates to the external principles guiding this commentary. As mentioned, the audience for a commentary is most important, and I assume an audience which may be generally unsympathetic with Hegel but somewhat conversant with the trends in analytic philosophy of history. Thus, what I have attempted on several crucial points is to construct Hegelian critiques of certain contemporary methodologies for philosophy of history, for example, Hempel's views on explanation in history. Obviously a Hempel-Hegel dialogue is anachronistic and, moreover, seems bizarrely inappropriate. Hegel is concerned, so it is assumed, with grand prophecies about the course of world events, while Hempel is interested in precise descriptions of the methodological principles of historiography. To force Hegel into methodological controversies may push the texts at times, but not as much as one might assume. In the preface to an article on one of the seemingly more exotic sections of the *Phenomenology*, the section on phrenology and physiognomy, a noted contemporary philosopher associated with the analytic school, Alasdair MacIntyre, argues most convincingly for the need of "reconstruction" in Hegelian commentary:

> *The Phenomenology of the Spirit* was written hastily. It is notorious that one outcome of this is that the arguments are compressed, that the relation of one argument to another is often unclear, and that paragraphs of almost impenetrable obscurity recur. The commentator is therefore liable to feel a certain liberty in reconstructing Hegel's intentions; and the exercise of this liberty may always be a source of misrepresentation, perhaps especially when Hegel's arguments are relevant to present day controversies. Nonetheless, the risk is sometimes worth taking.[11]

As he goes on to say, the reason for risking reconstruction of past philosophers in contemporary idiom is that "philosophical problems lie so close to permanent characteristics of human nature and human language" that we have strong warrant for assuming that even the most curious of past formulations may relate to the live issues of our own time.[12]

In sum, then, I have attempted to "fill in" the sketchy character of the text of *Reason in History* by appeal to the fundamental principles guiding Hegelian philosophy in general; at the same time, I have, when possible, reconstructed the arguments in terms which engage Hegel's views with those under active discussion in contemporary analytic studies of the philosophy of history. A final note: in searching for a vehicle for communicating Hegel's view of "world philosophical history," I have repeatedly resorted to a comparison between this kind of history and the views of history embedded in the history of science and the history of art. While some work has been done on the philosophy of the history of science, there is very little on the philosophy of the history of art.[13] The views which I offer of the history of those two fields are not to be taken as definitive or deeply developed, but they are views which have wide comprehensibility and currency so that they serve nicely as elucidatory devices for understanding Hegelian history.

It was said of Stirling's early commentary on Hegel, *The Secret of Hegel*, that if Stirling had discovered the secret of Hegel he had certainly kept it. I hope that this commentary will be a true elucidation of the central Hegelian ideas about history, but I sympathize with Stirling. Elucidation is almost necessarily simplification, and one must do some damage to the original in any commentary. Hegel's dialectic of historical consciousness is magnificently involuted and complex, and this commentary offers a rather flattened out version of his sinuous reflections. Nevertheless, to chart some main lines in a territory so nettled over with confusion is, I hope, a useful endeavor.

*Does Hegel Have
a Philosophy of History?*

Critical and Speculative Philosophies of History

Almost all recent accounts of the philosophy of history, particularly
those stemming from the analytic school of philosophy, divide the
subject into two quite disparate branches. W. H. Walsh states the
distinction and some of the reasons for its importance in his widely
used *Philosophy of History.*[1] He opens the volume by noting the
ill-repute into which philosophy of history has fallen. The chief
reason for the low estate of the study has been the predominance of
the European way of approaching the subject, a way typified by
Hegel. Walsh notes: "Philosophy of History, as practiced by [Hegel]
. . . thus came to signify a speculative treatment of the whole course
of history, a treatment in which it was hoped to lay bare the secret of
history once and for all." Walsh rightly concludes: "All this was
anathema to the cautious British mind."[2]

In order to restore the subject to favor, therefore, Walsh proposed
a distinction on the following grounds:

> I must point out the simple and familiar fact that the word
> "history" is itself ambiguous. It covers (a) the totality of past
> human actions, and (b) the narrative or account that we construct
> of them now. This ambiguity is important because it opens up at
> once two possible fields for philosophy of history. That study
> might be concerned, as it was in its traditional form [e.g., by
> Hegel] . . . with the actual course of historical events. It might on
> the other hand, occupy itself with the processes of historical
> thinking, the means by which history in the second sense is
> arrived at. And clearly its contents will be very different according
> to which of the two we choose.[3]

An earlier version of this chapter was published in *History and Theory*, vol. 10, no. 3,
copyright © 1971 by Wesleyan University. This use is by permission of Wesleyan
University.

Walsh labeled the two kinds of philosophy of history "speculative" and "critical" and concluded that "it needs very little reflection to see that a philosopher who rejects the first of these studies is not thereby committed to rejecting the second."[4] Virtually all textbooks and analyses which have appeared in recent years have echoed Walsh's distinction. To cite two examples:

> An introduction to the philosophy of history must begin by distinguishing two senses which the term "history" commonly bears. On the one hand we use it to refer to the course of events.... On the other, we use it to denote the historian's study itself.... Corresponding to these senses are philosophical disciplines, often referred to as speculative and critical philosophies of history. The speculative seeks to discover in history...a pattern or meaning which lies beyond the purview of the ordinary historian.[5]

> Philosophy of history may be divided into a critical part and a metaphysical or speculative part. Critical philosophy of history... is a philosophical inquiry into history considered as the scientific discovery and explanation of past human actions—that is, into "historiography.".... Metaphysical or speculative philosophy of history...endeavours to determine the meaning and purpose of history considered as the totality of past human actions.[6]

Having established the distinction, most of the practicing philosophers of history in the English-speaking countries make haste to abandon speculative philosophy of history in favor of the surer footings of critical philosophy of history.

In light of the philosopher to be examined in this book I would like to raise two problems with this commonplace of modern analysis. The first is the question whether such a distinction in method really exists as noted; second, even if one were to accept the distinction wholeheartedly, the question can be raised whether Hegel should be classified as a speculative philosopher of history—even though this classification has been universally agreed upon by all those who accept the two ways of doing philosophy of history.

First of all, it is interesting to note that none of the philosophers cited *argues* from the distinction in subject matter to the distinction in method. It seems to be assumed that it follows immediately from the observation about subject matter that there are two radically distinct ways of doing philosophy of history. Obviously, events and narrations of events are different; but are they so related or unrelated that wholly independent studies can be established for each? It is not my intention to argue this issue at length, but it is worth voicing some caution about the easy move from subject matter to method. Since the argument most frequently cited for the legitimacy of the distinction in philosophies of history is a parallel distinction in philosophies of science, it should be pointed out that the possibility of a nonmetaphysical philosophy of science is not without controversy.[7] If one takes Rudolph Carnap's work as a monument to the enterprise of a "logic" of scientific inquiry which would avoid all metaphysical claims, then the arguments raised against his position might give some pause to similar efforts to have a logic of historical inquiry free of all ontological assumptions.[8]

Without attempting more than a cautionary word about the move from subject matter to method, let me consider the effect which the distinction between two philosophies of history has on the evaluation of Hegel's work in this area. Consider Hegel's own comments:

> History combines in our language the objective as well as the subjective side. It means both the *Historia rerum gestarum* and the *res gestae* themselves, both the events and the narration of events. (It means both *Geschehen* and *Geschichte*.) This connection of the two meanings must be regarded as significant and not merely accidental. We must hold that the narration of history and historical deeds and events appear at the same time; a common inner principle brings them forth together.[9]

In this passage Hegel notes the difference in subject matter which is so crucial to the modern distinction in methods but appears to draw precisely the opposite conclusion. The course of events and narration of the course of events are linked as "subjective" and "objective," conjoined by a "common inner principle," and the conclusion that seems to follow from such a relation is that a radical separation in methods of philosophy of history would be inappropriate. *If* Hegel is correct in his claim that there is a common inner principle which links events and narrations, then the crucial distinction so central to modern views about the study of philosophy of history cannot be made. The issue between Hegel and his modern critics and commentators would then be more complex than is usually supposed. Hegel is universally regarded as a speculative philosopher of history, but it seems that from the standpoint of his own system no such philosophical enterprise can be derived. I am not trying here to justify Hegel's position but only to point out that the distinction which is so central to modern analyses apparently cannot be made in his treatment. What is taken as an almost unarguable commonplace by contemporary analysis would be regarded by him as a profound mistake. Hegel would be under no compulsion to defend the work of "speculative philosophy of history" since he recognizes no such philosophical method.

Hegel's position on the relation between events and narration is not immediately clear or defensible, and much of the second section of this chapter will be devoted to an elucidation of his position. There is a way of reading his views, however, which is easy to comprehend even if it may appear particularly wrongheaded. Consider his amplification on the matter of events and records:

> The periods, whether we suppose them to be centuries or millennia, which peoples have passed before the writing of history, may have been filled with revolutions, migrations, the wildest transformations. Yet, they are without objective history because they lack subjective history, records of history. Such records are lacking, not because they have accidentally disappeared through the long ages, but because they never could have existed.[10]

It seems to me that Hegel's position is perfectly clear (except perhaps for the technical terms, "subjective" and "objective," of which we shall hear more later), but it probably appears to most readers as simply false. We all know about "histories" of ancient people where we are sure that no historical narratives ever existed. These "histories" have been reconstructed by latter-day historians from religious records, potsherds, architectural remains, and so on—none of which could be regarded as "historical narrative." If one feels that Hegel's position is clear but false, it is important to see in what sense it is falsified.

Consider the following two statements:

      (a) This area had no inhabitants.

      (b) This area had no history.

Suppose we find some human artifacts in the area; in that case (a) has been falsified by empirical evidence. But what kind of evidence falsifies (b)? For Hegel, at least, it would not be the discovery that events did *in fact* take place in the area. He readily admits that there may well have been "revolutions, migrations, the wildest transformations," and yet he refuses to regard these deeds as evidence that the people had a history. Obviously he wishes to use the term "*historical* event" in a restricted manner which does not cover all human deeds. (If no such restriction is allowed, then (a) and (b) are equivalent, since if an area has human inhabitants it has human deeds and history.)

Again, without defending Hegel's desire to limit the notion of historical event to a subset of human actions, it is worth pointing out how damaging this restriction is to the common characterizations made about his philosophy of history. A general mark of speculative philosophers of history is that they deal with the "totality of past human actions," but it seems that Hegel claims to deal only with a designated subset of human actions.[11] The quarrel between Hegel and his critics should not focus on his *presumption* to deal with all human events but with his restriction of history to certain kinds of human events. If Hegel is wrong in his claim that there are no historical events without historical narratives, it is not because he is mistaken about the fact of human deeds in "prehistorical" periods, but because he wishes—for reasons to be discussed below—to withdraw the label "historical" from these events.

It is quite clear what subset of human actions Hegel wishes to regard as the proper subject matter of history—those events for which historical narrative exists. The criterion is both clear and applicable but a first glance appears singularly useless and misleading. In fact, one could argue that Hegel's putative criterion was precisely the one utilized in historical writing prior to the advent of modern historiography, and that example is sufficient to show the grave limitations of the proposed formula. A. D. Momigliano notes:

> To the best of my knowledge, the idea that one could write a history of Rome that would replace Livy and Tacitus was not yet born in the early seventeenth century. The first Camden Praelector of History in the University of Oxford had the statutory duty of commenting on Florus and other ancient historians (1622).... Both in Oxford and Cambridge Ancient History was taught in the form of a commentary on ancient historians.[12]

It was this kind of attitude which produced the historical compendia which R. G. Collingwood was to characterize as "scissors-and-paste" history.[13] The contemporary historian is absolutely dependent on extant historical records, and he can at best arrange them in a chronological sequence and comment on obscurities. If this is the kind of history that Hegel has in mind, then his views on history would not be overly ambitious, as his critics claim, but all too meager. Rather than exaggerating the ability of historians to find the "pattern of meaning" of history, he would be restricting them to the merest surface. The whole development of "critical" historiography—not to be confused with "critical" philosophy of history—would be negated.

In summary, then, I have attempted to raise the following problems about the conventional characterization of Hegel as a speculative philosopher of history: (1) Does the distinction between critical and speculative philosophy of history hold *in general*? (2) What possible meaning could such a distinction have in Hegel's own terms? (Answer: none.) (3) Even if one admits the legitimacy of speculative philosophy of history as a special method *and* agrees that Hegel's philosophy should be so characterized, it appears that he clearly deviates from the formula by dealing not with *all* human events but only with a designated subset. (4) At least one apparent way of reading Hegel's views on the proper subject matter of history would make his views on history both meager in scope and shallow in method rather than speculative and "profound." With these problems in mind, I will look in a more constructive way at what Hegel is attempting in his philosophy of history.

Original, Reflective, and Philosophical History

Having raised some problems about how to describe Hegel's task in *Reason in History* in the light of currently accepted distinctions, I propose to examine directly how Hegel derives his concept of "philosophical world history" or "philosophy of history" or "the philosophical method of history"[14] from an examination of two other methods of writing history, which he labels "original" and "reflective." My basic assumption is that the puzzling final method of writing history, the "philosophical world history" which he sees as his task, sums up and incorporates the insights of the previous methods discussed while avoiding their partialities and mistakes (Hegel's notion of a "dialectical synthesis"). This reading is certainly suggested by the Hoffmeister text, in which Hegel makes the transition to "philosophical world history." "The third style of history, philosophical world history, begins in this last reflective mode of thinking about history [*Spezialgeschichte* in German; "fragmentary history" in Hartman's translation] because its view of history is also universal."[15] He then goes on to contrast "fragmentary history" and "philosophical world history" as a movement from the abstract universal to the concrete universal, a move which normally announces for Hegel the culmination of a dialectical derivation of a given concept.[16]

If one is willing to grant that Hegel's new way of reading history by a philosophical method is somehow derivative from the previous methods, then one can gain illumination by examining his analysis of those other methods. The crucial analytic tool for understanding those other methods can be stated in various ways. What is at stake in these methods is the relation between the historian and the events which he writes about, or, in Hegel's own language, the relation of the spirit of the historian and the spirit of the times he writes about. In its most generalized Hegelian form, it would be regarded as the relation between subject (the historian) and object (the events). This distinction runs through his accounts of the various methods. Of original historians he says: "They primarily described the actions, events and conditions which they had before their own eyes and whose spirit they shared."[17] In contrast, he says about the reflective historians: "Here the main thing is the elaboration of the historical material. The historian achieves this with his own spirit, which is different from the spirit of the material."[18] We would assume, then, that in true Hegelian fashion he is pointing toward a new and higher synthesis between the historian and his subject matter in the third and culminating philosophical method. He describes philosophical history as reason contemplating reason, which sounds like a synthesis of some sort between investigator and investigated. "To him who looks at the world rationally the world looks rationally back."[19] The difficulty with this statement is that it seems either terribly wrongheaded or hopelessly obscure to most readers. I do not propose to dwell on it except to indicate that some kind of synthesis of "subject" and "object" is at work in the philosophical way of reading history.

Perhaps the most innocuous way of stating the analytic contrast that Hegel is concerned with throughout his investigation of methods of history is to describe it as the contrast between the historian and the events he writes about. It was suggested in the first section that one way of reading Hegel might indicate that he had a very naive view of history which would confine historical method to pasting together extant narratives. But the root distinction behind his analysis of ways of approaching history is the clear separation between the "spirit of the events" and the "spirit of the author."

This is nowhere made clearer than in his account of one of the submethods of reflective history: critical history.

> [Critical history] is the mode in which in present day Germany, history is written. It is not history itself which is presented here but rather history of historiography: evaluation of historical narratives and examination of their truth and trustworthiness. The outstanding feature of this method, in point of fact and intention, consists in the acuteness of the author who wrests results from narrations rather than events.[20]

In Hoffmeister's text the following is inserted parenthetically after the second sentence in the quotation above: "Niebuhr's *Roman History* is written in this fashion."[21]

If Hegel was thinking of Niebuhr's work as a significant kind of reflective history, then his overall vision of history could hardly be "scissors-and-paste." Since it is Collingwood who coined the notion of scissors-and-paste history, consider his account of Niebuhr and the German historical school:

> The historians of the early and middle nineteenth century had worked out a new method of handling sources.... This essentially consisted in two operations: first, the analysis of sources (which still meant literary or narrative sources) into their component parts, distinguishing earlier and later elements in them and thus enabling the historian to discriminate between more and less trustworthy portions; secondly, the internal criticism of even the most trustworthy parts, showing how the author's point of view affected his statement of the facts, and so allowing the historian to make allowances for the distortions thus produced. The classical example of this method is Niebuhr's treatment of Livy, where he argues that a great part of what is usually taken for early Roman history is patriotic fiction of a much later period.[22]

In his account of critical-reflective history, Hegel appeals to the root distinction between the spirit of the historian and the spirit of his times and indicates that a latter-day historian like Niebuhr, who is aware of a possible mismatch between the attitudes of the historian and the times he is describing, may win historical results from that realization.

A "critical" attitude toward sources is based on the possible discrepancy between the spirit of the author examined and the events described, the basic Hegelian distinction in his account of the methods of writing history. With this distinction in mind, then, we can examine the various complexities of relation between the spirit of the historian and the events he writes about as they are outlined in Hegel's account of the methods of writing history.

Original history presents an interesting and distinct problem for the latter-day critical historian questioning sources. Here the spirit of the historian and the events are said to be the same. Lest there be any dispute about this unity, we can take a pure case of original history, an autobiography such as Caesar's *Commentaries*, which Hegel classified as original history—"the simple masterpiece of a great mind."[23] In autobiography, "subject" and "object" are obviously the same. The life of the historian himself is at issue. Taken from the more sophisticated standpoint of the critical historian who considers the possible distortion between the attitudes of the author and the actual events, original history in the autobiographical mode presents a special problem. There is a sense in which no matter how one treats the autobiography *critically* we still gain historical results about the events described. A man may distort the events of his life consciously or unconsciously, but the fact of the distortion in this case reveals historical data about the subject matter which is his own life. There is no autobiography, however dull, distorted, or self-serving, which does not obviously reveal the author in some fashion.

In contrast, if we move to Hegel's reflective history, where the spirit of the historian and the spirit of the subject matter are divided, the subject is no longer the object. Then the intrusion of the historian's personal eccentricities, prejudices, or noble sentiments becomes problematic and probably distorting. In the ordinary garden-variety history, we expect to be told about the events in question, not about the historian who writes the book. The great dispute over the Beard-Becker thesis is precisely whether this kind of "neutral," self-effacing posture is possible for the historian, but the fact remains that such is the ideal of normal historical writing, even if it is judged to be only a "noble dream."[24] If we discover a distortion in a reflective history, we are not directly illuminated about the events described, although we may derive some information about the historian and *his* times. This latter investigation can be very interesting as part of the "history of ideas," in which the attitudes of a nation are traced through the attitudes that historians take in different periods toward a particular event in the past.[25]

I would conclude, therefore, that Hegel has pointed to an interesting and widely accepted consideration in making his initial distinction between original history and reflective history. Once we realize that the historian not only writes about events but also forms attitudes which are themselves historical events, then we have derived two different ways of looking at historical narratives. In autobiography, or what one might call "participant history" (to cover cases like Thucydides), the two phases merge, so that subject and object coalesce in what Hegel labels "immediacy." A reflective historian's attitudes are also historical events but not events of the times he writes about.

Noting the overall distinction between the two methods, let us turn to a delineation of the various subcategories of reflective history. Under the general umbrella of reflective histories, in which the historian's life and times are a different issue from the life and times he writes about, Hegel distinguishes, in order, four separate types: universal history, pragmatic history, critical history, and "fragmentary" history (*Spezialgeschichte*). It is the basic contention of my analysis that these four subcategories, in the order stated, constitute a dialectical development leading to the final step into philosophical world history. Problems raised in defining each of the methods force the argument forward to ever more reflective and sophisticated views of the nature of historical writing. The argument from this point, then, will attempt to reconstruct this line of development.

A historian is presented with Thucydides' account of the Peloponnesian War. Here is a narrative by someone who desires to preserve a record of events which occurred in his lifetime. The historian says to himself: "That is very interesting, but obviously this is only a partial picture since the man has confined himself to events with which he was in some fashion personally in contact—either as witness, or from reports of contemporaries, and so on. There is no inherent reason why history should be confined to the lifetime of a single witness; let us then expand the account beyond what Thucydides could himself have participated in either directly or indirectly and give an account of Greek history overall."[26] The move is then made directly from original history to reflective history in the universal mode. "The first kind of reflective history connects with original history if it has no other purpose than to present the totality of a country's history."[27] A "defect" of original history in terms of scope is to be remedied.

Two problems arise at once, however, when the historian moves from the framework of original history to reflective-universal history—problems which we can designate, following Hegel's general terminology, as "subjective" and "objective." On the objective side, what is the inner principle which limits scope? Is there any way in which we can treat only the history of Athens in the fifth century without doing the sixth and the fourth? And what about the history of Persia, and of the Hellenistic period, and of Rome, and so on, until we are compelled to write a world history? To use Hegelian terminology, we are forced to an "infinite" expansion on the side of the object. Indeed, there is something arbitrary in confining an account to the life of one man, Thucydides, but is there anything less arbitrary in any other confinement short of the whole of world history?[28] It is this expansion on the side of the object that causes this first kind of reflective move to result in "universal history."[29]

On the "subjective" side, universal history has a defect which is obvious from our previous discussion. "But the individuality of spirit which must characterize a writer who belongs to a certain cultural period is frequently not in accord with the spirit that runs through the period he writes about. The spirit that speaks out of the writer is quite different from that of the times he describes."[30] And at this point in the text, Hegel criticizes Livy along the lines of Niebuhr's evaluations. "Thus Livy makes his old Roman kings, consuls, and generals speak in the fashion of accomplished lawyers of the Livian era, which contrasts strongly with the genuine traditions of Roman antiquity."[31] The historian who is not, obviously, a participant in the events he describes may begin to be troubled by a bad conscience about whether he is really speaking about the past or subtly using historical materials to express his own present attitudes. As someone said of Charles Eliot Norton's lectures at Harvard: "They were lectures on modern morals illustrated by ancient art."

A historian who has passed to the stage of universal-reflective history begins to have qualms about the objective and subjective characteristics of such history. How monumental and impossible to write *universal* history, how difficult to capture the spirit of other ages! Seeing the problem, he makes a virtue of necessity and says: "Since I cannot write about everything, and I will probably reflect the attitudes of my own age anyway, I shall accept that fact and limit my scope and define my interests by my present concerns." He picks up, in other words, the opposite pole of the Hegelian subject-object dichotomy and determines his field on the side of the subjective. It is

the historian's own times and interests which become the principle
of selection for the writing of history, not a universal "objective"
history of the world. This kind of reflection moves us from the stage
of universal history to pragmatic history.

> Pragmatic reflections, no matter how abstract, belong indeed to
> the present, and the stories of the past are quickened into
> present-day life. Whether such reflections are really interesting
> and full of life depends on the spirit of the writer.[32]

Without being unduly anachronistic, one could say that this
Hegelian "pragmatic" history is very close in spirit and statement to
twentieth-century pragmatic theories of history as expressed by men
like Beard, Becker, and John Dewey. Since problems are always
present problems and since inquiry is the solving of problematic
situations, Dewey concludes:

> The slightest reflection shows that the conceptual material
> employed in writing history is that of the period in which a history
> is written. There is no material available for leading principles
> and hypotheses save that of the historical present. As culture
> changes, the conceptions that are dominant in a culture
> change.... History is then rewritten.[33]

> We are committed to the conclusion that all history is neces-
> sarily written from the standpoint of the present, and is, in an
> inescapable sense, the history not only of the present but of that
> which is contemporaneously judged to be important in the
> present.[34]

Consider Hegel's comment on pragmatic history in the light of
these remarks:

> One [pragmatic] reflective history, therefore, supersedes another.
> Each writer has access to the materials; each can think himself
> able to arrange and elaborate them and inject his spirit into them
> as the spirit of the ages. Weary of such reflective histories, one has
> frequently taken recourse to presenting events from all possible
> angles. Such histories are, it is true, of some value, but they offer
> mostly raw material. We Germans are content with them; the
> French, however, spiritedly create a present for themselves and
> refer the past to the present state of affairs.[35]

One might conclude from Dewey's and Hegel's accounts that
history has now returned at a higher level of reflection to autobiog-

raphy. (This is essentially the kind of skeptical stance taken by a "pragmatic" theorist like Becker in essays such as "Everyman His Own Historian.")[36] We are back at the state of "original" history in a more complex guise, since what is expressed is the spirit of the historian, and every historical work turns out to be a piece of the historian's biography now "mediated" opaquely through opinions on other people's lives and times rather than through the "immediacy" of autobiography.

This "return" to the earlier stage of original history is exactly the kind of development that one expects in a typical Hegelian analysis. Of course, it is not a literal return or retrogression to the earlier state. The "return" has the usual mark of such Hegelian returns in that we have recapitulated original history on the level of "the idea." All that means, simply, is that in reading the spirit of the reflective historian in a pragmatic history, we are not recovering great deeds and events, as in the case of Caesar's account of his deeds (or, on the subjective side, a Caesar's lies, self-deceptions, or higher aspirations); rather, we only get the latter-day historian's ideas, attitudes, and values. The value of pragmatic history would be measured by the extent to which the pragmatic historian really reflects something important in his *own* times. The "objectivity" of the history is given by its status as evidence for a vital current of thought in the times of the pragmatic historian.

One can trace in this progression the kind of dialectical movement which Hegel favors. First we posit autobiography in which subject (the historian's life) limits object (the historian's life recorded) or where subject and object are "identical." Because of the arbitrary limitation in scope which such original history necessitates, we are moved onto a "higher" level in which the objective scope is widened. But this immediately leads to problems with the subjective accompaniment of the spirit of the historian who writes such extensive histories, and we are driven back onto the subjective pole by the positing of pragmatic history in which the spirit of the historian in the present again limits the subject matter.

Having come full cycle back to the original historian, only on the "ideal" level, we should consider what has been accomplished by these reflections and how the historian should proceed (if at all) from this point. What has been accomplished by the sharp swing from objective expansion in universal history to subjective contraction in pragmatic history is that the two poles which were merged "naively" in Caesar's *Commentaries*, the life of the historian and the deeds reported on, the subjective and objective problems of historical writing, have now been brought painfully to consciousness. There appears to be a fatal division between the historian and the events—between subject and object—which had been innocently overlooked. From this point on in the discussion, the problem will be to reunite subject and object while at the same time preserving the insights gained from the analysis so far.

If original-universal-pragmatic marks one triplet in the argument, such that pragmatic history replicates on the level of mediation and "idea" the notion of original history, the last three methods—critical-fragmentary-philosophical—form a second triplet in which philosophical world history will recapitulate in a "higher" form the stage of critical history. The first triplet has brought the dichotomy of historian and events to self-consciousness; the second triplet begins by exploiting that self-consciousness of the dichotomy to gain historical results. As was noted above: "The outstanding feature of this method consists in the acuteness of the [critical historian] who wrests results from narrations rather than events." Once we realize that earlier methods of history were naive in not considering the effect of the historian's spirit on the account he is offering, we may use the fact and nature of the account itself as material evidence rather than report.

Another way of stating the move made by the critical historian is to say that he regards narrations *as* events, thus breaking down the dichotomy posed by the previous analysis. As events, narrations are direct, material evidence about a time; they are, one might say, a part of the time which is made present to the historian here and now. The main points to note, then, in the move to critical-reflective history are (1) the new "synthesis" of subject and object which comes about from regarding the attitudes of the narrator being criticized as an event, and (2) an irreversible turn in the progression of methods toward a consideration of ideational material (attitudes, values, views—in short, "spirit") as the primary subject matter.

The exact defects of critical history are not easy to discern from Hegel's brief and rather polemical text. Perhaps the crucial attack is contained in the following passage:

Here we have another method of gaining actuality from history: replacing historical data by subjective fancies—fancies which are held to be the more excellent the bolder they are, that is, the smaller their factual basis and the larger their contradiction with the most definite facts of history.[37]

The concept which stands out in this passage in the terms of the analysis presented in this essay is "subjective." The force of the criticism can be brought out by considering an alternate translation of the opening phrase, which can be rendered: "Here we have another method of bringing the present into the past"[38]—a comment which relates directly to the previously analyzed method of writing history, pragmatic history, which is decidedly present-centered history. The present that is brought into the past under critical history is regarded as merely subjective—it is not the *problems* of the present age that are used to organize historical research, as Dewey would have it, it is the bold fancies of the historian. One might regard the contrast as one between a truly *pragmatic* historian who must rethink history for actual, political needs of the day (objective needs), and the merely academic, critical historian who reconstructs the past only out of his own subjective views. The former's history has some grounding in the objective—so that we can use the political, pragmatic history as evidence of the present from which it is written—while the academic, critical historian may reflect nothing except his own "academic" whims.

As was pointed out above, critical history is the first of a dialectical triplet which culminates in philosophical history. As the first in that triplet it has certain resemblances to original history. At its worst, critical history tells us only about the mind of the historian; thus it is a form of autobiography but now a very uninteresting autobiography, since critical history is not written (probably) by great men in contact with the problems of their times. The critical historian, unlike the original historian, exists on the level of ideas rather than action. He writes about great deeds, he does not perform them. The question that critical history raises is, "How shall the historian correct his ideas so that they are not merely subjective and idiosyncratic?" The answer, as I see it, is to deepen and expand the fundamental notion already present in critical history: the history of history. The historian must place subjective notions of interpretation in a framework of other historians' thoughts in the course of historical writing. In this fashion his interpretive principles are expanded, and the subjective element is "neutralized" (a term of Herbert Butterfield's in his discussion of the value of pursuing the history of historiography).[39]

The transition, then, from critical history to the next stage of historical investigation presents a broadening of scope from the ideological perspective of a single investigator (which may well be present-centered and merely subjective) to an investigation of the general history of ideas. This "expansion" parallels, after a fashion, the expansion from the autobiographical focus on the actions of great men in original history to the general history of a nation or civilization in "universal history." The hope is that broadening the ideological perspective will eliminate subjectivity. But Hegel's treatment of "history of ideas" raises certain difficulties about the nature of that discipline which finally force him to the perspective of philosophical history.

Since history of ideas constitutes the transitional stage to our goal of an elucidation of philosophical world history, let me quote Hegel's characterization of the discipline virtually in full. (The text is annoyingly brief.)

> [History of ideas] forms a transition to philosophical world history. In our time this kind of conceptual history has been particularly developed and emphasized. Such branches of history refer to the whole of a people's history; the question is only whether the true context is made evident or merely shown in external relations. In the latter case they appear as purely accidental peculiarities of a people. But if such reflective history succeeds in presenting general points of view and if these points of view are true, it must be conceded that such histories are more than the merely external thread and order of events and actions, that they are indeed their internal guiding soul.[40]

The critical point that I wish to bring out is the transitional character of history of ideas between what has gone before and philosophical world history. The nature of this transition is suggested in the problem raised about whether such histories show "the accidental peculiarities of a people, merely external relations," or "the internal guiding soul" of events and actions.

If we accept the notion that "fragmentary history" is some form of the history of ideas, then it is possible to make sense of the text just quoted by considering two examples of history of ideas: history of art, which Hegel explicitly mentions, and history of science, which he does not, but which serves to illuminate partially the problem with which he is struggling.

History of Ideas

From a Hegelian standpoint, most histories of art are conceived merely subjectively, or only "in external relations." Histories of art tend to be chronicles of how tastes change over time. First there was impressionism, then post-impressionism, then the fauves and cubism, constructivism, and so on. Tastes and tempers change, and historical accounts note the chronology. Nor do we have to view this as mere chronicle. One could show how the post-impressionists reacted to the impressionists, or what the cubists took from Cézanne, or trace the import of some puzzling iconography. To Hegel this kind of history of art would still be "subjective" and a display of art only in external relations. To see this point more clearly, consider what it would be like to write the history of science on the model suggested for the history of art. At one time people believed that the world rested on the back of a tortoise, at another that it was flat; later they came to regard it as round. One might show that there were relations between the various stages: A's model of the tortoise-backed earth influenced B's notion of a flat earth; or we could note how religious notions influenced Kepler's research. The problem would be what *kind* of relations, and in the history of science these relations have an inner rationale. It was not that B got tired of the tortoise-backed earth and wanted to express some new feeling about space; rather, he rejected the earlier view because new evidence or a more comprehensive theory required the rejection of the earlier view. Kepler's religious interests are irrelevant to his value in the history of science. To write the history of science as the history of subjective opinion, even if one were to show how one subjective opinion influenced another, would be regarded as absurd. But why? Interestingly enough, a history of science along these lines might not contain a single false statement. The proper order of scientific opinions might be noted, as well as the "influence" of one scientific theory on another, and a history of world views would certainly be presented. But it is not science, one would reply. The author has all the data but he has missed the spirit of the thing. In the history of science we do not have a mere "external thread of ideas"; what we have is an "inner guiding soul." To write the history of science and miss the inner nature of scientific research as a cumulative, progressive verification and a falsification of hypotheses would be to miss the whole point of the history of *science*.

The history of science would appear to show certain peculiar traits which characterize Hegel's notion of fragmentary history. First of all, history of science is history of *ideas*, that is, the existential status of the field is ideational. Second, the history of science, while it exists *in* a subject as an idea, is not for that reason "subjective" in the pejorative sense.[41] The idea of science and/or the idea of the history of science involves a relationship between the various theories offered which is not merely accidental, subjective influence but shows an inner logic in which ideas of later periods include and confirm, or exclude and disconfirm, earlier notions. The rationale of the scientific investigator involves placing his theories into the ongoing development of science. To be sure, we think this "developmental" and "objective" component in the history of science is peculiar to that subject matter. Surely history of art (and probably that of morality and religion) is "subjective," and the relation of the ideas at different periods is one of subjective influence. There is no progressive realization of the "truth" in these areas. Hegel would be inclined to model the other histories on the one sketched out here for history of science, but that is not a controversy into which I will enter now. The crucial problem which I wish to clarify here is not how one views the history of art or morality but how one views the history of historical writing as a branch of history of ideas.

History of history is certainly a branch of the history of ideas and one to which some notable contributions have been made by men like Geyl, Gooch, Butterfield, and others. What if we pose the question raised by Hegel's account of fragmentary history? Does the history of history show the writing of history "only in its external relations" as the "purely accidental peculiarities of a people," or is there an "internal guiding soul"? If the history of history is written merely subjectively (as, we suggested, the history of art is normally written) then we could certainly note the influence of the times on the attitude of the historian and the influence of one historian on another; but in the long run history would fall under Santayana's dictum: "History is myth corrected by further myth." I believe that there are strong reasons not to regard the history of history on the subjective model. A historian of history who did nothing but note the changing values of historians over time would subject himself to self-referential refutation that he himself was after all only showing *his* values. While there are people who would be willing to take such a view (and not only about history but science as well), I think it fair to say that anyone who approaches the matter in that fashion simply does not understand the *idea* of historical writing—which is precisely to open up one's opinions to further correction over time. Beard and Becker would have defined a historian by his possession of "the noble dream," even if they thought it was only an unrealizable ideal; and Dewey, while seemingly very skeptical about historical writing, bases his whole "theory of inquiry" on progressive verification over time.

History of history would seem to be the crux of all other kinds of histories of ideas, including the history of science. Hegel says in beginning his discussion of the philosophical method of approaching history: "The sole thought which philosophy brings to the treatment of history is the simple concept of Reason."[42] One might justifiably reverse that and say that the sole idea which our investigations bring to the study of reason is the idea of history. The idea of history or historical consciousness is present in any context in which ideas are presented in a fashion which makes them *internally* vulnerable to further ideas which will develop out of the original presentation. This sense of development or internal "vulnerability" over time has a clear meaning when we talk about the history of science, but there may be other kinds of internal connectedness between ideational products which are similar to the development of science and which would do in other realms what the process of refutation and confirmation does in that area. Clearly, this is Hegel's view.

To view politics historically it is necessary that a group set up a constitution or set of laws which becomes a terminus a quo for later thought. The fundamental law seen as a historical object is subject to a kind of clarification, adjustment, amendment, and rectification or revolutionary overturn that would not be the case if the law is viewed as ahistorical, transhistorical, or part of "natural law."

The work of Mircea Eliade on "pre-historic" societies[43]—which govern the whole range of their life values on the basis of such myths as the myth of the eternal return—gives us some concrete idea of what it is like to live without historical consciousness. In such societies "revolutions" might occur, but they would not be regarded as revolutions in our "historical sense" as a point *from which* life was different in some fashion. All *new* events are excluded in ahistorical societies and are seen as mere repetitions of eternal patterns. A devout Hindu once assured me that television could be found in ancient scripture and referred me to the Ramayana, where Krishna is seen at two places at the same time. Ideas are presented in a historical context—whether they are scientific, artistic, political, or moral—only when they are subject to change at a later time by means which bear *directly* and *internally* upon the content of the original idea. A revolution in politics would be such an inner connection provided that it was more than a paroxysm of boredom. To be historically related, later ideas call into question either favorably or unfavorably the worth of the idea originally offered, and he who offered the idea must recognize this vulnerability in his presentation or he is not thinking historically. Any idea or attitude which does *not* contain such a principle cannot really be viewed historically. A subjective connection of ideas such as is generally accepted in the history of art really makes a historical presentation no more than a chronicle which is useful only for certain hermeneutic purposes. Picasso is influenced by Cézanne, and this knowledge may help us to interpret his works, but Picasso does not develop from Cézanne, correcting or expanding his vision. Truly, in art one might say that "every epoch is equally close to God." For Hegel, that amounts to viewing the matter ahistorically. Thus other histories such as those of morality or politics, viewed on the model of history of art rather than on that of history of science, are really only accidentally "historical." If one were to write such "histories," Hegel would say that they were perfectly correct, containing many true statements; all that they would lack is a sense of history. The historian would have all the tools except historical consciousness.

Hegel's move from consideration of the problems of the history of ideas to the nature of philosophical world history can be stated as a move from particular modes of historical relatedness between ideas to the problem of historical relatedness in general. Philosophical world history is, in effect, a history of historical consciousness. The task of the philosophical world historian is to note the development of historical consciousness in various times and places. At some times, historical consciousness may be rare and applied only in limited areas of human action; in other times it may be more central to the organization of subgroups or of the entire society or civilization. Hegel has his own opinions about where and how historical consciousness manifests itself, and I would not wish to defend his empirical views on these matters. But it seems to me that there is a prima facie case that such a history of historical consciousness is possible and would not be "speculative" or "metaphysical" in any negative sense. Historical consciousness as outlined in the account of the root attitude in history of science certainly has existed and can be clearly contrasted with other ways in which other ideas appear to be regarded, for example, the "history" of art.

If there is to be a history of historical consciousness, it must be written with historical consciousness—which means that it must be developmental. It must move toward "objectification" in some sense similar to the increasing objectification which is a central ingredient in understanding the history of science.[44] It is Hegel's insistence that historical consciousness as a subject matter for history must contain this internal connectedness, which we call "progressive," that has most outraged his detractors. How can we say that history progressed? How can Hegel say it, since he himself calls history "the slaughter bench at which the happiness of peoples, the wisdom of states and the virtue of individuals have been sacrificed"?[45]

I think that there are two ways of stating the position: a weaker and a stronger thesis. The weaker thesis would regard the statement "history is progressive" as an analytic definition of the nature of historical consciousness. Just as the nature of scientific thought is progressive in respect to history, so with historical consciousness. What that means is simply that when an idea is presented in a scientific or historical mode of thought it bears an internal connection to possible futures which will emend, or change, or incorporate the idea. Now, this is not to guarantee that anyone will actually pick up that option. It only means that this kind of correction over time is inherent in the way in which the idea is presented—it is a scientist publishing a theory, not an artist showing his canvas or a prophet announcing a revelation. Perhaps we shall grow bored with science and historical thinking in general and seek to live in the ideational framework of an eternal myth. As philosophical world historians we would say that historical consciousness is inherently progressive *if people choose* to play that game; but they may not, and it would seem that frequently the strains of historical thought have been too great, and people have lapsed into myth.

The stronger thesis on the progressive character of history asserts that historical consciousness has an ontological grounding and *will* assert itself. History is not a game human beings could choose to absent themselves from. This, I am sure, is Hegel's position. It is obviously much more difficult to defend than the weaker reading. If one denies that there is any "ontological" (Dewey would say "biological") grounding for historical consciousness, there are obvious problems about the genesis of such an ungrounded attitude. A mild suggestion at this point would be that insofar as men are defined as culture makers they are inherently historical, but that Hegel would restrict "historical consciousness" to the point at which men begin self-consciously to shape and mold their values (ideas) over time as they have shaped their flint axes and bone knives since time immemorial. We will return to this problem later.

World Philosophical History

The comparison between philosophical world history and the two modes of history of ideas—art and science—is a useful preliminary account of the direction of Hegel's argument, but it can be misleading if applied too literally. The account offered suggests too strong a similarity between history of science and philosophical world history to be wholly satisfactory. Natural science fails profoundly as a model for historical consciousness in Hegel, and so one must suspect that the history of natural science can hardly offer the model for Hegelian philosophical world history. This is a matter which we will examine in detail later on. Strictly speaking, in Hegel's own terms, what occurs in the development of the methods of writing history is a development of self-consciousness—a theme which is persistent in his writings and which has myriad ramifications. There are some relatively simple ways of seeing how this is so, however. In the case of original historians it is obvious that self-consciousness is central, since the original historian is writing either autobiography (an account of him*self*) or participant history (where his personal perceptions are part of the events described). The self-consciousness of original historians is "naive" or "immediate" in Hegel's terminology. They thought that they were simply transferring events from external reality into narration with no distorting effect from their own perceptions: "They [original historians] transferred what was externally present into the realm of mental representation and thus translated the external appearances into inner conception."[46] In one perspective this naiveté on the part of the original historian is entirely justified since the distinction made by latter-day critical historians between the spirit of the author and the spirit of the times fails to work for people whose own spirit is the subject in which we are interested. On the other hand, a scholarly historian must recognize that Thucydides is giving only his view of the Peloponnesian War; if we are interested in "the thing itself," we will have to go beyond the original historian's immediate, naive transfer of events into narrations.

The whole course of methods of "universal" history can be reconstructed as a progress in self-consciousness for the historian. What has been described above, in the examination of the failures of the various methods of writing history, is a kind of methodological sophistication of historical technique, a development of self-consciousness about the problems of writing history. In the process, the historian becomes acutely conscious of the possible distortions which his own self, his "spirit," may bring to the narration of historical events. What is particularly interesting about Hegel is that he refuses to stop where modern pragmatic historians stop and acquiesce to history as mediated autobiography—history which finally is grounded in the truth of the historian rather than in "objective" process. The key to his solution of the skeptical conclusion offered by pragmatic historians is contained in his analysis of self-consciousness itself.

Although it is the burden of the rest of this commentary to see how Hegel's views of self-consciousness intersect with his philosophy of history, one can at least state his thesis at this point. The trouble with the pragmatic historian—either as Hegel describes him or in his modern versions—is that he fails to appreciate the essentially *social* character of self-consciousness. If self-consciousness is finally private and personal consciousness, then the interference of self-consciousness, the necessary infusion of the historian's spirit into his narrative, will always lead back to private subjectivity and one's view of historical narrative will be relativistic and skeptical at best. For Hegel, however, levels of self-consciousness are functions of social and cultural forces which go well beyond the standpoint of the private person. To be self-conscious is not to be personal and isolated but to live deeply in cultures which evaluate men and events in certain distinctive modes. The thread which runs through the consummatory triplet of methods of history—critical history, *Spezialgeschichte*, and world philosophical history—is the progression from self-consciousness as private and idiosyncratic (critical historians) through the self-consciousness of a people through the world historical view of the self-consciousness of many peoples in their dialectical linkage. The practitioner of philosophical world history is intensely *self*-conscious and his work is in a sense the description of that self-consciousness. He resembles, as is appropriate in Hegel, the original historian who merely translates his self-consciousness into mental concepts, but where that was a naive, immediate gesture on the part of the original historian it is an eminently cultured, educated self which expresses its inner life through the mediation of world history. The philosophical world historian has an intense self-consciousness because he has understood the modes of self-consciousness present in the cultures of the past. His self-consciousness is molded by "styles" of consciousness in the past, he incorporates their partial insights into his and arrives at a true self-consciousness which is more than the eclectic compilation of views which Hegel says is the final resting point of pragmatic historians. The philosophical world historian writes the history of history, the history of historical consciousness, the history of self-consciousness as the method of universalizing his own self-consciousness.

Obviously there is much more that has to be said about the nature of self-consciousness and the nature of history if the thesis stated above is to be made comprehensible or plausible, but I hope that even at this point it is possible to detect how dialectical development runs through Hegel's account, in the 1820 preface, of the methods of writing history. It is very important in assessing Hegel's achievements (or failures) as a philosopher of history to understand as clearly as possible the nature of the intellectual task he set for himself. As indicated in the first section of this chapter, that task has been misunderstood, in my judgment, and what I have attempted is a corrective. One must ask, "What is the nature of philosophical world history as Hegel develops it?" rather than coming with some preconceived view about "metaphysical" or "speculative" philosophies of history. Philosophical world history is the sum of the other more conventional methods, and it corrects the partialities and distortions of those methods. It is like original history in that the historian shares the "spirit" of his subject matter only this sharing is not naive and immediate but cultivated and mediated. The philosophical world historian is the supremely *reflective* historian who writes *as* a historian about historical consciousness (merging of subject and object). His work is *universal* in the fullest sense since it is world history, the whole march of historical consciousness, and it is *pragmatic* in the sense that he writes out of his own present and self-consciousness but now a self-consciousness which is the cultivated product of the historical process. Surely the Hegelian historian is a *critical* historian since he describes critical history as "the history of history." But unlike the academic scholar who is a mere critic of texts, the Hegelian world philosophical historian sees the very distortions of the past as part of the ideological struggle of peoples to define themselves and to advance the understanding of human reality.

To discover critical discrepancies and correct the distortions of past historians without seeing at the same time the struggle for human self-definition that is the basic raison d'être of historical writing in the first place, might well be taken as the definition of the historical pedant. Distorted history, the discovery of the critical historian, may be the very meat of historians of ideas who convert the factual error into spiritual truth if they link the "distortions" to the inner life of a people coming to comprehend itself. Once one realizes that the thrust of all genuinely historical writing is the struggle for social self-consciousness and that this struggle is transferred from people to people, from culture to culture, then one has attained the stance of the philosophical world historian and is prepared to write Hegelian history: the history of historical consciousness.

3   *Objective Reason*

The Second Outline of 1830

In the previous chapter I attempted to reconstruct the character of "world philosophical history" as a dialectical development from the other methods (*Arten*) of historical writing which Hegel outlined in two series of lectures given in 1820 and 1828. In 1830 he offered a "Second Outline" which attempts to characterize the task of the philosophy of history more from general philosophical considerations than from any survey of the actual methods of historians. In Hartman's translation from the second edition of Karl Hegel the two sets of lectures are melded together so that one is not aware of the fact that manuscript materials from different times have been compounded. This editorial composition is not a fatal fault; the two outlines do not contradict one another in basic doctrine, but the manner of approach is different. I will use the change in approach offered in the Second Outline as a point of departure for a further attempt to characterize Hegel's views on the task of a philosophy of history.

My major interest in this chapter (and in the entire commentary) is the famous quotation about reason as the "law of the world" which occurs very early in the 1830 manuscript material. But before getting to that grand thesis, Hegel offers some general comments to his philosophical auditors about the task of philosophy of history which are worth noting. To summarize the argument of the short, three-page introductory remarks: Hegel says that he assumes everyone understands well enough what world history is all about, but what a *philosophy* of world history is may require some explanation and justification. He then offers the bland notion that philosophy of history is nothing more than the thoughtful contemplation of history (*die denkende Betrachtung*).[1] After all, he comments, it is precisely thinking that differentiates men from animals, and if thought is the necessary ingredient in other human activities then certainly it should be present in human history. But this raises a problem about the character of philosophical thinking and historical thinking.

> In history, thinking is subordinate to the data of reality which later serve as a guide and basis for historians. Philosophy on the other hand, allegedly produces its own ideas of speculation without regard to given data.[2]

This consideration immediately raises the danger of the philosopher writing a priori history, which is precisely the charge that has so often been raised against Hegel since his time. It is a charge he is at pains to deny, but his final position is not immediately clear.

He defends the autonomy of philosophy in philosophy of history by noting that historical thinking is, after all, not as "passive" as one might at first suppose. One could, of course, simply gather up the data in an "unmediated" fashion, but everyone agrees that such simple compilations do not constitute historical thinking; one must at least search for the "causes and grounds of events."[3] He further goes on to note that thought is present in historical thinking for making logical connections: "For those things that are to be deduced from history, everyone recognizes that logical thought is necessary."[4] So far, one could easily agree, but then he makes a statement which seems peculiarly Hegelian and puzzling:

> Philosophy [contrary to the model of merely logical deduction] understands something quite different by the concept; here conceptualization is the activity of the concept itself, it is no mere concurrence of matter and form which has come from somewhere else.[5]

He goes on to say that although pragmatic history can be satisfied with mere concurrence of matter and form, philosophy (philosophical world history?) cannot: "it essentially takes its matter and content from itself,"[6] and in this there appears to be a real conflict between historical thinking, which relies on what happens, and the self-generating character of the "concept." He closes these introductory remarks with two paragraphs emphasizing the seeming contradiction between the autonomy of philosophical thought and the dependence of historical thinking on facts, "external necessity," natural conditions, and so forth. To show how this opposition between philosophical thinking and historical events is resolved in philosophical world history is the task of his own investigation.

A full elucidation of Hegel's views on the relation of philosophical thinking and historical thinking is the overall task of this commentary, but a useful preliminary understanding of the rather obscure comments about "the concept" can be obtained by comparing even this brief Hegelian characterization of the relation of philosophy and history to one of the most interesting and persuasive of contemporary theories, C. G. Hempel's views on explanation in history. Because Hempel's views exemplify a mode of philosophy of history which is so decidedly different from Hegel's, I will refer to it often in this commentary. Hempel's theory has been central to analytic discussions of philosophy of history both as an object of defense and attack, and it is a theory of great power and intrinsic merit. For all these considerations, I will outline the theory for the benefit of historians or the ordinary reader who may not be as well acquainted with it as most professional philosophers.

Hempel's views on explanation in history can be stated briefly and simply since they are models of philosophical lucidity.[7] Hempel argues that historians obviously are not mere compilers of "facts," they also "explain" facts. Historians explain the cause of the Civil War, the results of the last election, the fall of Rome; they do not merely describe the facts attendant on those events. In this, Hempel obviously agrees with Hegel that the historian's task is not merely to lay the facts before us in an "unmediated fashion" but to search for grounds or causes. Hempel would also agree with Hegel that historians have to use logic in deducing conclusions, but for Hempel the logic of deducing conclusions in history is really all there is to historical explanation. Hempel's thesis is frequently called the "covering law model," and it asserts that what constitutes an *explanation* in history is nothing more or less than being able to deduce a singular statement from the conjunction of a general covering law (major premise) and a statement of initial conditions (minor premise). The example that Hempel offers as a model explanation is the account one might offer for why an automobile radiator cracked on a certain cold night. The major premise states general laws about the behavior of water under certain atmospheric conditions, the strength of radiator materials, and so on. The minor premise states that the temperature on this night was such and such, that the radiator was indeed made of these materials, and so on. From the statement of the general laws and the initial (particular) conditions, I can logically derive the singular statement that this car radiator cracked. Hempel has modified and sophisticated this account in many ways—particularly by the inclusion of statistical laws as candidates for the major premise—and the central thesis and its sophisticated versions have been subjects of controversy and very fruitful philosophical discussion. I do not want to enter into the ramified versions of Hempel's thesis; rather I will remain at the simple statement of it, which has a classic persuasiveness.

Hempel's general view, then, of historical thinking can be summarized as follows:

> (1) Historians do not merely describe events.
> (2) Historians also explain events.
> (3) The only possible notion of explanation is the deductive covering-law model.

Hegel obviously agrees with (1) since he rejects any notion of historical thinking which would make the historian a mere passive receptacle of fact. He agrees with Hempel that historians must tie the events together, mediate them, and that this is an activity of "thought." What Hegel would deny, however, is that the mediating device is "explanation" according to the covering-law model. I discuss later on in this chapter why Hegel might reject the precise notion of explanation as such for the conceptual ligature of historical thinking. But at this point I want to state briefly what Hegel would find particularly objectionable in the Hempel program: the assimilation of "thought" in historical work to "logical deduction." The power of Hempel's views on explanation is that they seem to be based on the necessary logical structure of thought. If historians explain events (and it seems they do), what could possibly serve as explanation except strict deductive necessity? In this, Hempel's later modifications of his theory to include statistical laws seem somewhat unfortunate, as Alan Donagan has pointed out.[8] Statistical laws don't explain singular events, they only yield a probability that they will occur. We know there is a probability that I will get measles, but why did I get them here and now? Hempel argues for the inclusion of these statistical laws because of the fact that they are used by natural scientists, but the real power of his theory of explanation lies in the fact that it appears to rest on the logical necessities of thought rather than on the practice of scientists.

Hegel was generally unimpressed with merely formal systems such as logic, and he even has some harsh things to say about the intellectual value of mathematics. For Hegel, analysis of form abstracted from content was valueless. As he says about art, "There is not only classical form there is also classical content,"[9] and we will examine later on his strictures against merely "formalist" treatments of history. From his standpoint the application of formal logical considerations as the key to *historical* mediation is seriously misconceived. To be sure, historians are not illogical—they do not violate the canons of argument—but what is peculiar to the way in which history is put together is not something which it shares indifferently with logical thinking in general or with the natural sciences in particular. For Hempel the problem of the philosophy of history is no different than the problem of explanation in the natural sciences, and explanation in turn is nothing more than application of the canons of deductive thought—at least in the pure theory of covering law. For Hegel such explanation is the mere concurrence of matter and form which finally fails to understand the nature of the subject. History presents a peculiar subject matter, and as such it requires a particular "logic of historical thinking" as we would say today. The logic (form) of historical thought must be commensurate with the peculiarities of historical subject matter.

While Hempel and Hegel disagree basically about the mediating structures for historical data, both defend the autonomy of philosophy in determining that structure. Hempel's theory about explanation in history is a prescriptive theory about historical methodology. One of the major anomalies of Hempel's theory, as his critics have been quick to point out, is that it is virtually impossible to point to actual cases in which historians offer covering-law explanations. Nor are practicing historians entirely pleased when Hempelians point out this failure in method. Many practicing historians say that not only do they not use covering-law explanations but they have no intention of doing so—after all, philosophers really don't understand what history is all about anyhow. Hempel is not constructing a priori history (deducing the battle of Waterloo), but he is certainly practicing a priori historiography in deriving the proper conceptual tools for historians from general philosophical considerations. His "concept" for history, explanation by law, is not inductively derived from actual examples of historians' work; it is generated autonomously from fundamental philosophical considerations about science and rational thought.

A different approach to philosophy of history would be for a philosopher to take his cue from the actual work of historians and propose a "descriptive logical geography" of the field rather than a prescriptive methodology. Although philosophers occasionally claim to be doing just that—merely mapping the logical geography of study or field or term—one is hard pressed to accept this claim. Mere mapping would be a peculiarly fruitless task for history. Historians are by no means agreed themselves on how history is to be structured, and anyone purporting to map the field of historians' practice ought not to be obliged to accept every self-proclaimed historical method. Any investigation of the logical geography of history will establish some norms if only by majority vote of the practitioners. Hegel in his lectures of 1820 and 1828 examines various "methods" actually used by historians and derives the "proper" world historical methodology from them—not by an eclectic gathering of principles but by a dialectical examination of their strengths and weaknesses. No one would suppose, however, that Hegel simply found these methods well formulated at hand. The methods discussed are obviously purified forms derived from an overall conception of what he *already* projects as the proper nature of historical consciousness.

Hegel shares with Hempel, then, an approach to the philosophy of history which has a distinctly a priori element; more accurately, neither philosopher is willing to surrender an autonomy of philosophical examination of history to a mere inductive mapping of practices of people called historians. Hempel is not at all perturbed, evidently, by the fact that actual historians fail to accept the need for his kind of explanation in history. His challenge must be that if they don't offer this kind of explanation then they simply are not doing history in the sense of a "science" trying to give understanding to human events. They may compile facts like archivists or cataloguers, they may construct romantic narratives which please the reader, but if history is to be taken as a rational discipline it simply must explain events and that by using covering laws. To Hegel, Hempel would not be wrong in prescribing proper historical method to historians, but he would be mistaken about what is properly *history*. The limit of Hempelian prescription as far as Hegel would be concerned is "Be logical!" since Hempel's theory of historical explanation amounts to no more than an application in historical materials of general laws of thought. But the peculiar form of *historical* thought is matched to the special matter of historical investigation, and, for Hegel, Hempel would never reach that problem at all.

If Hegel wishes to be more than a logician prescribing laws of thought to historians, where does he derive his notions of the properly historical? Hempel's position seems eminently more defensible. Most people accept the notion that philosophers are particular experts in logic and the forms of thought, but why should they be experts in history as such? Hegel was supposed, after all, to have deduced the (wrong) number of planets from purely philosophical considerations, and if he was that far off as an astronomer, by what right can he lecture historians about what is the properly historical? A historian might grudgingly accept the notion that he didn't know much about logic and forms of explanation, but Hegel in his criticism of the various methods of historical writing is in effect telling everyone from Thucydides to Ranke that, finally, they didn't understand the real nature of their field. The major difficulty in coming to understand Hegel's position as a philosopher of history is that the "analytic" view of philosophy in general (and philosophy of history in particular) is one which he would reject. He may have been wrong to do so, but it is important to realize how and why he rejects the unstated assumptions of much of contemporary philosophical practice.

Although a modern philosopher like Hempel, or others who practice analytic philosophy of history, would be unhappy about the tortured phraseology in which Hegel states the autonomy of the philosophical concept, they could certainly accept the notion that logical concepts are autonomous, self-justifying products of strictly philosophical reasoning. The philosopher of history does not surrender his mastery of the (logical) concept to the historian. What saves the modern analytic philosopher from the accusations of a priorism that have descended on Hegel is the notion that the philosopher is after all, only prescribing the *form* of historical writing; he is saying nothing about the actual facts. The general picture of the philosopher in analytic circles is that he is some sort of logician (whether formal or informal is a matter of keen dispute) but that, clearly, he does not interfere with the substantive work of physicists or historians. When Hegel claims an autonomy of the concept derived from philosophy for the fundamental understanding of history, the very best that a contemporary analyst could do for him would be to grant him the status of a formal logician. But it is perfectly clear that Hegel is not content with such a formal role, and thus it is assumed that he has inappropriately meddled in the substantive business of historians. As we noted above, his general view of philosophy rejects the kind of form (formalism, logic)-matter (substantive science) distinction that is a commonplace of modern analysis. I have already examined this rejection in the special case of the distinction between analytic and speculative philosophies of history, and it is appropriate to see that rejection as of a piece with his general view of philosophy. In this respect, history is of primary importance.

As Hegel himself notes in the introductory remarks to the 1830 lectures, nothing appears more irresolvable than the autonomous thought of the philosopher and the dependence of the historian on the "given"; yet it is that resolution which he wishes to set forth in his investigations. When Hegel demands the autonomy of the philosophical concept over history, it must be understood that he has already rejected any formalist view of philosophy which would necessarily entail the incompetence of philosophy to deal with historical matter. For Hegel, the *philosophical* concept, properly understood, is nothing more than actual *history*, properly understood. This is the message of the final sentences of the *Phenomenology of Spirit*. The goal of that investigation has been to reveal the Absolute Concept (*der absolute Begriff*):

> The goal, which is Absolute Knowledge or Spirit knowing itself as Spirit, finds its pathway in the recollection of spiritual forms as they are in themselves and as they accomplish the organization of their spiritual kingdom. Their conservation, looked at from the side of their free existence appearing in the form of contingency, is *History*; looked at from the side of their intellectually comprehended organization, it is the *Science* of the ways in which knowledge appears [that is, phenomenology]. Both together, or History (intellectually) comprehended [*die begriffne Geschichte*] form at once the recollection and the Golgatha of Absolute Spirit.[10]

Admittedly, the exact doctrine of this passage is by no means clear, but the passage makes one thing plain. Hegel's view of philosophy and history is that in some strange way they coincide. Thus it is not really appropriate to accuse him of being an a priorist, as if philosophy, a wholly ahistorical discipline, was somehow to dictate to the historian. He views the properly philosophical concept as in some way a deeply historical concept. To assert the autonomy of philosophical thought and the dominance of "the concept" over the mere practice of historians must be understood, then, in the peculiar view which Hegel has of the task of philosophy. If one reads the normal "formalist" assumptions of twentieth-century philosophy into Hegel's remarks about the philosophical concept, his entire project is misunderstood from the start.

I have not attempted here to justify Hegel's views about philosophy and its unusual relation to history, nor do I imagine that they are entirely clear to most readers, I merely wish to sketch out how one must understand Hegel's general views about philosophy in assessing his remarks about the task of philosophy of history. Further elucidation and such justification as can be mustered is the aim of this commentary. The key to that elucidation is the famous passage which occurs next in the text on the role of reason in history.

The General Concept of History

Hegel's introductory remarks have claimed that history is not merely passive fact-gathering but involves thinking. The form of thinking that is peculiar to history cannot be identified with merely general forms of thought such as the logician may deal with; there is a peculiar kind of mediation, a peculiar mode of thought that is appropriate to historical work. This peculiar form of historical thought is known by the philosopher not by an inductive collation from historical practice but because he, somehow, understands the fundamental nature of historical existence. It is now incumbent on Hegel to describe the nature of historical thinking, what is it that transforms history from fact-gathering to genuine historical consciousness. A modern philosopher like Hempel tells us that what mediates the historical data is explanatory laws; Hegel has another candidate—reason.

> The sole thought which philosophy brings to the treatment of history is the simple concept of Reason: that Reason governs the world and that in world history things have come about rationally. This conviction and opinion is a general assumption in the consideration of history as such. In philosophy it is not merely an assumption; there it is proved through speculative knowledge, that Reason.... is both *substance* and *infinite power*, in itself the infinite material of all natural and spiritual life as well as the *infinite form*, the actualization of itself as content. It is *substance*,

that is to say, that by which and in which all reality has its being
and subsistence. It is infinite *power*, for Reason is not so
impotent as to bring about only the ideal, the ought, and to
remain in existence outside of reality—who knows where—in
the heads of a few people. It is the infinite *content* of all
essence and truth, for it does not require as does finite activity,
the condition of external materials, of given data from which to
draw nourishment and objects of its activity; it supplies its own
nourishment and is its own reference. It is its own exclusive
presupposition and absolutely final purpose, and itself works out
this purpose from potentiality to actuality, from inward source
to outward appearance, not only in the natural universe but also
in the spiritual—in world history.[11]

The explication of this single passage is the main task of this entire
commentary. I quote the passage almost in full not only because it
enshrines the central claim of Hegel's philosophy of history but
because it is so typical of the kind of extraordinary assertion which
has made his work notorious. A more immediate reason for quoting
the passage in full, however, is that the italicized words (the italics
are Hegel's) suggest an underlying structure of analysis which can
aid in understanding the passage and the whole of *Reason in
History*. The words are "substance," "power," "form," "content,"
and they are used in a passage which leads to the claim that reason is
"the absolutely final purpose" of history, working itself out from
"potentiality to actuality." Any general philosophical reader will
immediately recognize the vocabulary as Aristotelian. Under slight
disguise we can see the doctrine of the four causes: efficient cause
(power), formal, material (content), and final. In addition, there is
the general claim that reason is the "substance" of history and the
reference to the Aristotelian language of potentiality and actuality.
This could be merest coincidence, since Aristotelian terminology is
rather common philosophical coin even among philosophers who
may not recognize their borrowings. In the case of Hegel, however,
one can suspect that the italicization is meant to consciously remind
his readers of the Aristotelian matrix of causes. It is a well-known
fact that Aristotle was the philosopher from the tradition who had
the most profound effect on Hegel. G. R. G. Mure has not only
documented this fact but written two introductions to Hegel which
trade heavily on the Aristotelian background to illuminate Hegel's
view.[12]

The extended statement quoted above lays down the fundamental doctrine which Hegel will be defending in the rest of his work. As I will point out in chapter 5, the Aristotelian framework is the basic structure which governs the course of his argument as he considers in turn reason as end, power, matter, and form. Each of the subdivisions of the text (which appear to be Hegel's own) take up in order the claims set out in terms of the causes until he has given an extended analysis of the initial thesis. Before proceeding to the causal aspects of reason in history, however, Hegel discusses reason as the *substance* of history and it is here that we can begin to gather some notion of the general sense in which he uses this crucial term. As he points out toward the end of the section which begins with the long statement about reason: "One always speaks of Reason without being able to indicate its definition, its content, which alone would enable us to judge whether something was rational or irrational. What we need is an adequate definition of Reason."[13] For anyone who makes such far-reaching claims about reason and history (or for anyone commenting on the claims) this wish for a definition is eminently sensible.

The section which begins with the great quotation about reason is entitled "Its [World History's] General Concept." In that section Hegel makes a number of general points about the precise meaning of reason in history by contrasting his own views with other notions which might well be taken as either antagonistic to his or basically similar. From an examination of these arguments one can gather a fairly clear picture of the special sense in which Hegel is claiming that reason is "the law of the World." In analyzing these crucial passages I will utilize two devices. In the first place, I will assume that the Aristotelian language of the initial quotation is not mere accident and that a basically Aristotelian view of certain key terms is involved in Hegel's explication of reason. I am not assuming that the reader is particularly conversant with Aristotle, nor do I claim that my occasional interpretations of Aristotle are the last word in Greek scholarship. Basically, I believe that Hegel's use of certain key distinctions can be defended as common sense but that Aristotle, who is often thought of (well or ill) as the philosopher of common sense, may help to give some philosophical polish and depth to the argument. The basic value of using Aristotle here is not to make a scholarly point about the provenance of Hegel's views but to show how the assumption of a basically Aristotelian world view helps to make Hegel's arguments more comprehensible. The justification for thinking that Hegel held certain "Aristotelian" positions on the terms discussed turns on what he actually says in *Reason in History*, not on any putative influences of Greek philosophy.

The second device I mean to use in dissecting these passages is a distinction between what I will call "objective" and "subjective" reason. This is a distinction which is not supported by any explicit Hegelian dictum but which is implicit in the discussion of history and is constantly utilized in the development of the argument. The simplest justification of the distinction is to point to Hegel's specific reference to the two senses of history as "subjective" and "objective," the *historia rerum gestarum* and the *res gestae* themselves, narrations and events. Since we also know that he regards reason as the sole notion for history, it seems to follow that one could properly talk about reason in subjective and objective senses. As a matter of fact, Hegel does just that. There is a whole line of discussion about reason as a principle in certain objective, ontological processes like nature, and there is another whole stratum of discussion in which the "categories of Reason" are contrasted with such subjective, "mentalistic" notions as understanding or sense-perception. Hegel passes back and forth between these objective and subjective considerations of reason without taking any notice of the transition, and philosophers who wish to make hard-and-fast distinctions between objective and subjective, world and mind, events and narrations will be troubled by his failure to note the shift. It is, however, Hegel's basic thesis about history that subjective and objective are bound together by a common inner principle, so that for him the passage between these two ranges of discussion is immediate and natural. Nevertheless, for purposes of illumination in this commentary it seemed valuable to make a tentative separation between the two ranges of reason while keeping in mind that finally they must be made to coalesce in a single view of reason in history. The current chapter, then, will examine "Objective Reason."

Chance, Nature, and Spirit

A careful reading of the section on the general concept of philosophical world history which begins with the extended quotation on reason as the end, form, matter, and so on reveals three contrasts and comparisons which Hegel makes on the "objective" side of reason: chance, nature, and providence. The first contrast is to chance. In Hartman, it reads "One ought to have the firm and invincible faith that there is Reason in history and to believe that the world of intelligence and self-conscious willing is not abandoned to mere chance."[14] In Hoffmeister's text chance is dismissed in a passage from the *Nachschriften* immediately after the autograph quotation about reason in history:

> Philosophical investigation has *no other aim than the removal of chance. Chance is the same as external necessity, i.e. a necessity which falls back on causes which are themselves only external circumstances.*[15]

The first contrast then to reason in the events of history is to "chance" or "the accidental." At this juncture the reader may feel that he understands what Hegel is claiming but that the claim is unacceptable. The claim may be unacceptable, but the precise point which he is making is not as obvious as it may seem. Behind this simple contrast there is an implied "metaphysics" which must be made explicit before the claim can be properly evaluated. Whatever Hegel's own special views on metaphysics may be, it seems that in stating his opposition to chance he is relying on distinctions which are worked out in Aristotle—distinctions which, in general, are also those of ordinary language.

The contrast pointed to in the statement on chance is a contrast between some sort of causality which is merely external (chance) and a causality (reason) which is internal. What is the meaning of this external/internal contrast? One famous discussion of "chance" utilizing these terms is contained in the second book of Aristotle's *Physics*, in which he is treating of the character of changes which occur by *physis*, by nature. "Nature" he defines as an internal principle of motion or growth in the thing to which it belongs primarily.[16] The progress of a seed from bud to flower to bush (to use a Hegelian example) is a process which occurs *by* nature. There is an internal principle in the seed which necessitates the path which it follows in its growth. Aristotle contrasts this with the case of a doctor who heals himself. The doctor is not thereby cured by nature (assuming that he ministered properly to himself in a truly effective manner) but by the art of medicine. The fact that the same man is both doctor and patient is a mere external connection, and thus self-doctoring is not a case of a process going forward *by* nature. From the standpoint of Aristotle's discussion of natural change, it is very easy to distinguish natural processes from events which occur by accident, by chance, by art and so forth. Common sense and ordinary language follow Aristotle (or perhaps he followed them) here, and we think we can readily distinguish between the natural growth of the bush, the effects which the ill-chance of bad weather had upon it, and the special form into which the gardener's art has trimmed it.

This brief account of Aristotle's views helps to make clear in what sense "chance" can be regarded as an external cause, but if we were to leave the argument at this point it might seem that the internal principle or cause in history which Hegel calls "Reason" is none other than the natural causality which is Aristotle's internal principle of change within a process. Hegel is obviously aware of this possible error, an awareness brought out in Karl Hegel's text when Hegel turns immediately from his appeal not to abandon the world to mere chance to a comment on Anaxagoras.

> Anaxagoras...was the first to point that *nous*, understanding in general or Reason, rules the world—but not an intelligence in the sense of an individual consciousness, not a spirit as such. These two must be carefully distinguished. The motion of the solar system proceeds according to immutable laws; these laws are its reason. But neither the sun nor the planets...have any consciousness of it. Thus, the thought that there is Reason in nature, that nature is ruled by universal, unchangeable laws, does not surprise us; we are accustomed to it and make very little of it.[17]

Thus, while reason in history refers to an "internal" cause, it cannot properly be identified with causes "by nature."

The passage attacking Anaxagoras is typical of the blending of objective and subjective senses of reason. Reason is said to be manifested in natural law (the objective order of things), but finally reason has to be self-conscious (a "subjective" consideration); thus reason in nature won't suffice for Hegel's purposes. In Hoffmeister's edition, the entire section is structured very differently. After the rejection of chance as external causality, the text makes a number of interesting comments on the fact that it is professional historians who are the real a priorists (particularly the "critical" historians), and there is a discussion of the role of understanding in history (which we will discuss in the next chapter). Then Hegel turns abruptly to a development of the proper categories for historical process and offers an extended analysis of "objective" reason in history.

> The categories according to which the notion of history in general presents itself to our thought can be given quite quickly. The first category presents itself in the view of alterations in individuals, peoples and states—those who exist for a while draw our interest to them and then disappear. This first category is *change* [Veränderung].[18]

If one were to remain simply at the category of change, however, Hegel says one would not yet have derived the precise concept for history. One might, for instance, never make the distinction between internal and external causes of change. If that were the case, history would become a vast show, a kaleidoscope of ups and downs which, Hegel notes, we might react to either with a kind of aesthetic delight at the variegation of deeds and passions, with a moral sadness, or finally with boredom. The two paragraphs which follow the designation of the category of change as the genus of history evoke the charms and melancholy of history. These "aesthetic" views can be regarded as history seen as the changes of chance and external causality: history as mere spectacle, without pattern. Obviously mere external change will not do for "serious" history. (A wrong view of how events objectively tie together in history, or in this case fail to tie together, is accompanied by a wrong "subjective" value on the part of the person who views history. The two go hand in hand. This mismatch of a historian's values and the course of truly historical events is a constant theme in Hegel.)

Rather than abandon history to a melancholy view of the passing away of all things, Hegel says that reflection on that view of history indicates that there really is something further to be added to the notion of change: "However, there is another side to this category of change—that from death new life arises." He cites the well-known story of the phoenix as the type of "natural life" which is continuously preparing its own funeral pyre from which it arises "new, rejuvenated and refreshed." In contrast to this principle of natural life, we have the life of "the Spirit," causality according to reason proper, which does not simply repeat itself but which "elaborates upon its own existence; its embodiment becomes material for its work to elevate itself to a new embodiment."[19] While nature and history (spirit) contrast with chance or external causality, in that they both are understood by means of an inner principle of change, spirit or history has an inner principle which yields a pattern in change which is "progressive" rather than repetitive. This contrast between nature and spirit or between natural change and historical change is reiterated many times in Hegel, and it always rests on the same distinction. To take just one quotation from *Reason in History*:

> Historical change, seen abstractly, has long been understood as involving change toward the better, the more perfect. Change in nature, no matter how infinitely varied it is, shows only a cycle of constant repetition. In nature nothing new happens under the sun and in this respect the multiform play of her products leads to boredom. One and the same permanent character continuously reappears, and all change reverts to it. Only changes in the realm of the Spirit bring forth novelty. This appearance in the realm of Spirit allows man to see another determination than exists in mere natural objects... namely a capacity for real change and, to be sure, as we say, toward the better, toward the more complete.[20]

The importance of this repeatedly stated Hegelian distinction between reason in nature and reason in history, between natural change and historical change cannot be overemphasized. In many ways it is the crucial distinction in the entire analysis of history as a peculiar mode of being and a peculiar manner of thinking, and yet it is one that many astute commentators seem to have missed entirely. To take one of Hegel's most persistent and distinguished modern critics, Karl Popper: Popper accuses certain philosophers of history (whom he rather confusingly calls "historicists") of attempting to predict or prophesy the future. Hegel is seen as an archetype of the historicist mentality, and Popper says that this notion that we can predict in history is based on a confusion between natural systems and historical process. Popper says that for some *natural* systems "long term prophecies can be derived... if they apply to systems which can be described as well isolated, stationary, and recurrent. These systems are very rare in nature; and modern society is surely not one of them."[21] In the light of the distinction we have just drawn between nature and spirit in Hegel this criticism seems most inappropriate. It is not entirely clear that Hegel really thought he could predict the course of history—his remarks on America as the land of the future about which he can say nothing suggest he did not regard prediction or prophecy as his bent[22]—but it is absolutely certain that he did not confuse history with "closed repetitive systems." It is precisely this distinction between the closed, repetitive system and the "progressive" realm of the spirit that is the fundamental distinction between nature and history. Hegel may be completely wrong to fancy that there is any such thing as "spiritual" determination, but at least he clearly does not think that he is recasting historical studies on a model borrowed from the natural sciences. Popper's criticism might apply to Spengler, who seems to take rather literally the notion of a birth, maturation, and death in history (biological categories), but despite Hegel's occasional resort to similar terminology, his root notion is that causality by nature is an internal principle of change which is repetitive and hence cannot be a model for history.

It should be clear in what sense we have been discussing "objective" reason since we have been talking about characteristic patterns of certain events. Some events are connected only externally, and we call this "chance"; other skeins of events seem to be tied together as the unfolding of some inner principle in the change which we call "nature." Patterns of events regarded as the manifestation of nature are repetitive, and they are to be contrasted with another pattern of events which is internal to a series but which is progressive and introduces novelty. This is *historical* process. There is one final category necessary, though, for the proper description of the nature of historical process. Having said that history is change according to an internal principle of progress, one asks "Progress toward what?" If we look at the spread of historical incident and the "terrible sacrifices of spiritual content," we are compelled to search for a final purpose. "These observations lead us to the third category [of historical process], the question of a final purpose [*Endzweck*] which is in and for itself. This is the category of Reason itself."[23]

The general definition of reason in historical events (objective reason) is now complete: history is a process of *change* according to an *internal* principle which is *progressive* toward the realization of reason as an end which is final and self-justifying (in and for itself). The introduction of the third category of an end in history leads Hegel to the final subject matter of the section on the general concept of world history: providence. Since providence also postulates the end of history it is appropriate for Hegel to turn to that subject. The remainder of the section contains an extended discussion of this religious notion and Hegel's attempt to distinguish his views on reason in history from traditional notions of providence. We can come to a clearer understanding of the sense in which historical process must be defined as a progress toward reason by examining Hegel's discussion.

History and Providence

Hegel is trying to develop a notion of *historical* events as events which have an internal, that is, nonchance, connection which is unlike the internal connection that natural law or nature gives to events. He believes that an example of this kind of connection occurs in the traditional doctrines of providence. Hegel's own philosophy of history has many resemblances to traditional religious doctrines, and his own closing words in *The Philosophy of History* suggest the strongest possible identification between his philosophy of history and divine providence.

> That the History of the World, with all the changing scenes which its annals present, is the process of development and realization of the Spirit—this is the true *Theodicea*, the justification of God in History. Only *this* insight can reconcile Spirit with the History of the World—viz., that what has happened and is happening every day, is not only not "without God," but is essentially his work.[24]

The resemblance between providence and philosophy of history in the "speculative" mode is commonly assumed, and it raises particular problems in the interpretation of Hegel. Despite his own disclaimer that his theory rests on no special religious beliefs, many readers will assume that he is trading on unacceptable religious notions to carry conviction. Hegel's exact relation to Christian orthodoxy is a vexed question. Despite the rather anti-Christian tone of his early writings (misleadingly collected under the title of *Early Theological Writings*),[25] he evidently considered himself in the later years, when he was writing his works on history, a Christian. A later commentator like Kojève, however, considers Hegelianism the apotheosis of atheism, and I believe that there is a "secular" interpretation of *Reason in History* which depends in no direct manner on postulates of dogmatic faith. In developing the secular meaning of Hegel's search for a "meaning in history" it is useful, however, to see why he thinks his doctrine resembles the traditional notion of providence.[26]

In developing the notion of providence Hegel refers again to the two categories of chance and nature discussed in the previous section. His own view of reason in history is like the doctrine of providence insofar as providence is "the form of religious truth [which holds] that the world is not abandoned to chance, to external contingent causality."[27] He then goes on to specify the particular focus of his interest by saying that people have been willing to see providence at work in nature but have denied its effectiveness in history. It is only the latter category that concerns him, and he gives us a fairly typical example of the kind of situation which frequently is given a "providential" interpretation.

> In particular cases, it is true, one allows [providence] here and there, when pious minds see in particular events not only chance but God's will—when for example, an individual in great perplexity and need gets unexpected help. But these instances are limited to the particular purposes of the individual. In world history, the "individuals" that we have to deal with are peoples; they are totalities which are states. We cannot, therefore, be satisfied with what we may call this "retail" view of faith in Providence.[28]

There is a slight but interesting textual discrepancy here which can serve as a point of departure for comprehending the issues involved in Hegel's discussion of providence. In the Karl Hegel text and in Hartman's translation from that text quoted above, providence is said to be "not only chance but God's will" (*nicht bloss Zufälliges, sondern Gottes Schickungen*).[29] Hoffmeister's edition from Hegel's manuscript reads that pious souls see in these events not only God's general providence but his particular purposes: "where others see only the actions of chance" (*wo andere nur Zufälligkeiten sehen*).[30] The Hoffmeister edition appropriately sharpens the issue: one sees the event *either* as chance *or* Providence, depending on pious predilections. Providence is a form of nonchance causality relative to the career of an individual. Hegel accepts that definition in general but differentiates his treatment from the view of "pious souls" by noting that the "individuals" he is interested in are "states" or *Volk*. The passage suggests that there is a kind of intellectual "choice" here: either one sees an event as merely a matter of chance or one sees it as providential. What is interesting to note is that if we remained with the Aristotelian categories of nature and chance there would be no option, the event would have to be regarded as chance. The reason for this is that in the Aristotelian view the *object* of providential causality, the individual relative to whose life this event is seen to have purpose and meaning, is a mere chance occurrence. It is the emergence of *individuality* as a nonreducible, rational category which makes historical change (and providence) something more than natural change and chance.

In Hegel's view, as long as we stay at the level of natural change, the existence of the individual is wholly subordinated to the existence of the species or, as he calls it, "the universal." A naturalist who writes the "history of the whale" is not interested in the individuals he examines except as instances of the type. The history of the whale is a history of the species, not of named individuals. From the standpoint of nature and the naturalist, the individual repeats the type, and anything which calls attention to the particularity of this individual runs contrary to the interests of the scientist and the "interest" of nature in preserving the type. Hegel judges that in *real* history (not natural history) we are not interested in the individual as a repetition of a type but as something new and different. At one level, Hegel's search for progress and novelty in history is an attempt to avoid repetitive natural models for history. Hegel is searching for an internal order to a set of events which is different from the reinstantiation of the universal in the life of various particular instances. What is historical (or providential) is an event in the life of an individual which cannot be accounted for by natural cycles or relegated to mere chance.

One can rephrase Hegel's search for the final end of history (providence) by asking whether the meaning, function, or purpose of human beings as *individuals* is exhausted in what they contribute to the natural continuance of the species or whether there is some rationale that they have just *as* individuals. If we are left simply with the categories of Aristotle's *Physics*, natural change and chance, then the individual as individual falls into the category of mere chance. It is chance that I study this whale rather than another in writing the natural history of the species. This must be the case because if *this* individual differed from others in the biological group, my study would be devalued. The fact that providential views of history convert events which would normally be regarded as mere chance into events with an inner rationale relative to the life of the individual gives providential views a certain formal similarity to Hegel's attempt to rescue the status of the individual's particular career from assignment to chance. From the standpoint of the internal order of nature, the careers of individuals qua individuals *are* events of mere chance. For providence and history the individuality of things has an inner meaning which escapes from natural determination.

History takes as its subject matter individuals—they are the objects of historical change and process; the truly historical event must bear an internal relation to the character of these individuals. If "individual" was merely a piece of logical grammar which pointed to the metaphysical distinction between particulars and universal species, forms, or properties, Hegel's point here would seem very empty. "Individual" for Hegel is a "value loaded" term and is properly applied only to human beings and then only when they attain to certain kinds of self-understanding. For Hegel, only free, self-conscious, *rational* beings are truly individual. To say that historical events are concerned with the activities of individuals necessarily implies that history must be understood as rational, since only rational beings have any value as individuals.

Recapitulating Hegel's view of "objective reason" in historical events: history is generically categorized as *change*; it is not mere chance but change with an internal principle of order. This internal principle of order is not to be confused with nature, where the internal principle replicates the species, reinstantiates the universal. History is nonrepetitive and progressive, genuine novelty occurs. Novelty cannot be something merely different—some sport or variation from past patterns; it will have to be a newness which proclaims a relevant change in the forms of the past. In the language we have been using, genuine novelty has an internal relation to other events in the skein of happenings which makes up a genuinely historical sequence. A repetitive pattern in events is a form of understanding which precludes any valuing of individuality as such—the individual exists only as a means for continuing the species, the universal repeated pattern. If historical process is progressive and involves true novelty, then it is because there is something of value which lies beyond repetitive instantiation. If individuality as such can have a value, if individuality is itself an end (and in Hegel's mind *the* end), then we have located the proper subject (substance) of historical change.

What Hegel's philosophical view of history or, more accurately, what his notion of the properly historical process or mode of understanding shares with providential views is the "belief" in the meaningfulness of individuals and their careers. The historian who properly comprehends the nature of his field shares with the providential theologian the notion that individuals are comprehensible entities—neither accepts the view of the natural scientists that the dimensions of individuality, all that makes up *this* person and his career, is mere chance in the face of the intelligible form or universal. Where Hegel parts with traditional views of providence is on the proper individuals of history—for him these are not persons but peoples. In addition, he rejects the most conventional construction of providence as a transcendent explanation of historical events. Much of the long discussion on providence is taken up with criticism of traditional views which wish to leave a belief in providence merely formal and empty—there is a providence but man cannot know it. Hegel argues that this is contrary to the explicit injunction of the Bible to know God, and he points out that in the Christian religion God has revealed himself, so that that he is no longer hidden and secret. The upshot of this polemic is a justification of Hegel's view that the end or meaning of history is *in* history; it is immanent in historical process, not something which occurs beyond historical events in some other world. (This is the basis of Kojève's contention that Hegel is atheistic.) If the end is *in* history, then it seems we should be able to grasp it here and now in a concrete manner and not leave the question of history's meaning, purpose, or final end to a matter of empty, pious speculation.

One can restate the immanentist view of providence in a fashion which prescinds almost entirely from theological notions. What Hegel is insisting on here is some "analytic" relation between the proper subject matter of history (the bearer of history) and the meaning of historical existence (the end of history). Only free, rational beings are truly individual since only they have self-consciousness, which is the core concept of individuality. Individuality is a function of rationality, and vice versa. The "providential" question of what the meaning or aim of history is can be restated, "What is the meaning or purpose of individuality?" Hegel's philosophy of history is not, as I pointed out in chapter 2, a search for the meaning of events simpliciter, it is a search for the meaning of events which we "choose" to categorize historically *or* individually *or* rationally—to him such categorization repeats the same notion from different perspectives. A search for a final purpose in history shifts back and forth, then between "subjective" and "objective" poles: "What is the purpose of thinking historically at all (developing an intelligible category of history or individuality as opposed to nature and chance)?" and "What is the meaning of history (what is the function of individuality)?"

I don't believe that one can quarrel with the fact that Hegel obviously sees the proper subject matter of history to lie in "individuals," since he states his interest in states or *Volk*, the proper historical individuals, repeatedly in *Reason in History*. Anyone generally acquainted with Hegel may wonder, however, whether this interest in individuals is wholly consistent with his general rejection of particulars as being at all intelligible, which he makes at various places in the *Phenomenology*.[31] Hegel may *say* that he is interested in "individuals," but can he mean by "individuality" anything at all like what we mean—however hazily—in ordinary language and be consistent with his general reputation as an archrationalist, a thinker who reduces the data of history to the passing of ghostly forms? Hegel's views on the problem of particulars, universals, and individuals are exceptionally murky since they seem to cross all categories in an incomprehensible blur. If one turns to the final pages of the *Phenomenology*, Hegel attempts to categorize absolute knowledge (which we have noted is somehow bound up with history) by discussing its proper object:

> The object is, then, partly immediate existence, a *thing* in general—corresponding to immediate consciousness; partly an alteration of itself, its relatedness (or existence-for-another and existence-for-self), *determinateness*—corresponding to perception; partly essential being or in the form of a *universal*— corresponding to understanding. The object as a whole is the mediated result or the passing of universality into individuality through specification, as also the reverse process from individual to universal through cancelled individuality or specific determination.[32]

Anyone searching for a straightforward doctrine of the proper object of absolute knowledge (or history) from that passage is bound to be disappointed. Universal and individual are somehow seen passing into one another in ways that are not at all easy to comprehend. I will return at an appropriate time to a direct excursus on "individuality" as a Hegelian category, but for the time being I ask the reader to accept the notion that in some sense Hegel sees history as properly interested in "individuals" and that murky passages such as the one above indicate that even in his highly developed views individuality remains a vital category in whatever strange linkage it may bear to other important terms. When we turn to the development of what I call "subjective reason," we will gain some further ground in spelling out Hegel's proper notion of individuals and their importance for philosophy of history.

A Metaphysical Excursus; An Empirical Challenge

Before turning to the development of the notion of subjective reason, I wish to make a digression in order to examine in further depth some Aristotelian assumptions which seem to me to lie behind Hegel's development of historical process or objective reason in history. The two aspects I wish to explore turn on a metaphysical quarrel about the proper interpretation of "nature," and the empirical challenge which the theory of evolution creates for anyone who holds to the notion of fixed repetitive speciation. The digression illuminates the general view of Hegel's philosophy of history, in my judgment, but the discussion is more or less independent of the immediate line of commentary on objective reason.

It is generally admitted that Aristotle's notion of nature enshrines common sense—we do in everyday garden-talk make the distinctions about our plants which parallel the Aristotelian conceptions. However, to a more sophisticated view this resort to common sense may count against Aristotle. Surely we must have a more accurate use of such a crucial term as "nature" than common sense can discern or that rests on Aristotelian physics! Indeed, and it takes very little thought to discover a serious rival to this ordinary view of things. If we think again about the category of chance or accident, we may decide that chance is, after all, only a name for our own ignorance. The event which we regard as chance is as strictly necessitated to come about as the so-called natural development. It is chance, we say, that the tree was struck by lightning, but we know that the generation of lightning and the path which it follows is strictly determined by causal laws which are as predictable in theory as the laws which govern the growth of the acorn to the unfortunate oak. One could believe that common sense (along with Aristotle and Hegel) is simply incorrect to label one series of events those which occur by nature (growth of the oak) and the other set something that occurs by chance (striking of the oak by lightning).

The issues here are extremely deep and far-reaching, and it is not my intention to defend the Aristotelian-Hegelian use of "nature" beyond indicating what is involved in the way in which the term is regarded and how this choice affects Hegel's approach to rational causality in history. A view of "nature" which differs strikingly from common sense and conforms more to sophisticated theories of physics is found in Kant, where nature is defined as the totality of events connected by laws.[33] Under this view of nature—which is better capitalized "Nature"—the misleading notion of chance is removed, since Nature constitutes a universal system of causality. All events come about under law-like conditions and form part of the total system of Nature. Indeed, for Kant, the only possible meaning for an event which did not come about "by Nature" would be a miracle, and scientific men can have no use for such conceptual mysteries. So pervasive is this notion of Nature and the uniform, general causality of Nature that Kant was faced with the immense problem of trying to save human freedom as a causality which was not, he believed, "by Nature." If human moral action were part of the system of Nature, then Kant felt it would be impossible to ascribe responsibility to men for their actions any more than one could blame the lightning for destroying the tree. Even this brief sketch of Kant's view indicates its power and plausibility, but there are problems and implications in such a view that are disturbing.

Perhaps the major philosophical problem with such a view of Nature is that it appears to convert "nature" from a scientific term into a metaphysical one. In contemporary views stemming from Wittgenstein, a term is "metaphysical" and hence meaningless when it functions *without any determinate contrast.* Kant's "sophisticated" use of "Nature," which appears to run counter to common sense, is in considerable danger of misfunctioning because there are now no events or sequences of events which could be regarded as coming to be by Nature as contrasted to anything else. The Aristotelian and common-sense notion of what happens "by nature" is embedded in a rich group of contrasts: events that happen by chance, by art, by habituation, and so on. In Kant's extended designation of Nature in the universal sense, the only contrast he can point to is the perilously derived concept of human freedom.[34]

Kant's views on many matters have been rejected by contemporary philosophers, but there remains a kind of Kantian background to philosophy of science which has subtly influenced the discussion of problems of philosophy of history. For Kant, natural science constitutes the domain of what we can know in a strict sense, which is an assumption shared by philosophers like Hempel who come out of the positivist movement in twentieth-century philosophy. More important, however, the idea of "nature" in most contemporary analysis tends to be basically Kantian. For Kant, Nature is the totality of events connected by causal laws, and knowledge consists in properly ordering the causal chains. For Hempel, the problem of explanation in history is like the problem of explanation in the natural sciences, and, though the problem may be given a more linguistic tone, it remains one of explaining events by finding appropriate general laws. The important point is that the metaphysics of these systems is one which is structured around two central notions: event and law. Nature is the system of events according to law. Putting aside the fact that "nature" seems here to be functioning as a transcendental, that is, as a metaphysical term like Being, which is truly said of everything and hence puzzles us about its descriptive value, it is useful to note that the concentration on a system of Nature comprised of events according to laws is a strikingly different way of approaching the physical world than Aristotle's. Wittgenstein is a good Kantian when he opens his *Tractatus* with the metaphysical assertion, "The world is the totality of facts [events], not of things." This dictum runs counter to Aristotle's metaphysical views, which would have alleged just the reverse. Aristotelian physics pictures a world in which there are many *things* with different *natures*, and the problem of science is to discover the natures of these things and state them in a definition. The two notions of proper "science" are thus strikingly different: Aristotle—definition of the nature of things; Kant and the modern concept—explanation of events according to laws. For Aristotle there are, as it were, many natures according as there are truly different things in the world; for Kant and the modern view there is one nature, which is the system of events unified by law.

Aristotelian science is supposedly a discredited enterprise which sought the explanation of the narcotic effect of opium by noting its dormitive qualities. This is hardly the place to try to resurrect Aristotelian physics, but if I am correct that Hegel's philosophy of history was developed within a framework of Aristotelian conceptions then it may be valuable to see how these basic notions should affect our reading of the text. Hempel and most of his critics and supporters assume that the task of science, and of history as a particular case of science, is explaining events by laws, so when they turn to Hegel they are likely assume that he too is interested in explaining historical events by some sort of "spiritual" laws. But if Hegel is being Aristotelian, he is not basically interested in explaining events by laws at all. In Hoffmeister's index the word *Gesetz* appears twice and both times it refers to the legal machinery of states. If one looks at what Hegel actually does in the historical sections of philosophy of history, it is much more plausible to see him practicing Aristotelian "science." What we get are attempts to characterize (define) the spirits ("natures," "essences") of various peoples (the "things" of history). To be sure, as we pointed out above, Hegel is very concerned to radically distinguish *historical* substance from natural substance so that the problem of defining the "nature" of peoples is a fundamentally different task than the definition of species in nature. Nevertheless, the historical process takes off from a contrast to the Aristotelian natural process, and the historian's task is contrasted to the job of Aristotelian naturalist.

If one pursues some of the arguments which incline philosophers toward a law-event metaphysics rather than a definition-substance metaphysics, it is possible to see why Hegel could have thought of himself as genuinely empirical in his interest in history and how he might well turn the tables on his modern, positivistically inclined opponents and accuse them of the very sins with which he has been taxed: a priorism and metaphysical mysticism.

The principle difficulty of the law-event model—at least in its Kantian framework and for some positivists who follow him—is that it yields a kind of monism which in turn leads to "metaphysical" reduction of appearances. Aristotelianism as a bureaucratized branch of common sense maintains a delightful pluralism of reality. There are many things and systems with different natures. In Kantian views there is just the one nature and all multiple things are simply parts or moments in the great whole. Chance, for instance, is mere appearance; if we knew better we would see the strict necessity of the whole system that led to the fracture of the oak by the lightning blast. Indeed, human choice in super-monists like Spinoza is also illusion from the standpoint of *Deus sive Natura*—the one, only, and ultimate substance. The internal/external contrast which Hegel uses to banish chance as a principle in history is revealed in monists as mere appearance. The many things, the many actions of everyday life quickly are absorbed into the mighty view of monistic nature proceeding to spin out events according to law. If I am right that Hegel works within an Aristotelian understanding, then he too is a pluralist who does not reduce everyday diversity to the overall machinations of spirit. By and large, Hegel has been regarded as a monist who continually uses an appearance/reality distinction to devalue the everyday in terms of the mystic One, but I agree wholeheartedly with J. N. Findlay, when he says:

> It was Bradley, not Hegel, who believed in some Absolute Experience within which the objects of our ordinary human experience would be unbelievably fused and transformed, in which ordinary categories would be done away with without being replaced by anything that *we* can hope to understand. . . . [The English Hegelians] make use of contradictions to abolish the world of appearance and the notions of ordinary life. . . . In Hegel, however, the apparent and false are *retained* in his final result whose content is, in fact, no more than the clear understanding of the process which has led up to that result itself.[35]

Strangely enough, under the interpretation offered in this commentary, it is the positivists who in their metaphysics of knowledge are the mystics and Hegel who is the man of plural, common sense.

The pluralism of a "natures" metaphysics assists Hegel in many ways. In the first place it makes it relatively easy for him to regard nature and history as two essentially different realms. He is in no danger of confusing natural history and human history, as some of Hempel's critics have accused him of doing. For Hegel it seems obvious that there are different kinds of processes about in the world; nature is one and history another. His problem is to explain the "nature" of history in a way which clearly distinguishes it from the "nature" of nature. The pluralism also helps to explain the way in which he actually goes about writing his philosophy of history. If the problem of world philosophical history is to be truly "scientific," that is, to find a proper internal order in events rather than a mere "external thread," then Hegel sets about it in good Aristotelian fashion by detailing the various natures of the various peoples. In terms of the modern controversy which has centered on R. G. Collingwood's work, Hegel would see the scientific problem of history as one of finding insides. He would agree that once we know what happened (what is the nature of this people) we also know why it happened, so that the search for causal laws is not necessary. From the Hegelian standpoint the modern Hempelian program for scientific history is too speculative, since it would attempt to find laws which would connect *all* events in a single, overall theory. (Hempel, after all, holds allegiance to the great positivist search for a unified science encompassing all knowledge in a single deductive model.) But this would seem as bizarre to Hegel as the man who can't discriminate between the things that are—natural or historical objects with "insides": ducks, drakes, and dynasties—and the things that aren't at all—mere accidental collections and orders. What we are interested in are the various things that take on shape in the world because they have an internal principle of comprehension, they can be seen as *something*: natural objects or historical individuals. Perhaps a superdemon or a superphilosopher could run *all* the events that happen, accidents and all, into some superorder, but that seems theoretically suspect and practically useless. It is, at least, not the task of philosophy of history.

This discussion of "nature" and "by nature" has been relatively extensive because it is the contrast between nature and spirit (reason) which is central to an understanding of Hegelian history. It is all too easy to suppose that "spirit" is the problematic term and that we understand nature quite well. What I have attempted to show is that certain ways of construing nature make the basic Hegelian contrast impossible to draw.

In closing this chapter we turn to an empirical challenge to the whole Aristotelian-Hegelian framework of nature. It appears crucial to Hegel's distinction that nature repeats itself, that the species is fixed and that the individuals are mere instances of a type. It is in contrast to this static view of nature that he can point to the realm of the spirit, which is progressive and developmental. What happens to this Hegelian view when the theory of evolution of the species gains ascendancy? Aristotle, the greatest biologist of the ancient world, has been repeatedly taxed for his static view of species, and it seems that Hegel deserves no less criticism.

This is a very tangled issue to which only a very superficial treatment can be accorded. One could resort to the necessities of ordinary language. Granting full weight to the theory of evolution, there is no doubt that it has very little effect on the gardener's view about what comes about in his garden by nature, by art, by accident, and so forth. No view of the mutability of species can overlook the time scale on which this occurs relative to the life of a human observer. More important, however, one must note evolutionary pressure for the *persistence* of successful adaptation. Species change, but they change as species, that is, a new pattern for multiple repetitions is set up. To say that species change is not tantamount to dissolving the structure of organic nature into a flux, an unstable show of forms. Hegel could rework his view by saying that nature strives toward forms which can successfully be repeated, while spirit never repeats itself but is always "progressive."

One could perhaps defend Hegel by saying that the theory of evolution shows that spirit really does triumph over nature in the long view. The law of species is the law of spirit since species are not static and repetitive but changing and developing. Some theorists like Findlay actually claim that evolutionary theory vindicates Hegel by showing that historical categories are not exclusive to human affairs but apply to nature as well. I think that this would be a very poor defense for Hegel and I am reasonably certain he would reject it. There is a passage in Hoffmeister in which Hegel faces the problem of evolution almost head-on and which gives us insight into the kind of change that characterizes history. He says:

> In nature, the species makes no progress, in the realm of the Spirit however, every change is progress. To be sure, the series of natural forms constitutes a progression [*Stufenleiter*] from light up to men so that each successive step is a transformation of the former, a higher principle produced through the sublation and decline of the former. In nature, however, all this breaks down and all the individual branches remain existing alongside one another; the transition appears only to the thinking mind that conceives of the connection. Nature does not comprehend itself and therefore the Negative is not present in its forms. In the spiritual sphere on the other hand it happens that the higher forms are brought forth through the recasting of the previous, lower forms. The latter have ceased to exist therefore.[36]

In this passage Hegel admits that there is a scale of nature in which each form leading up to man successively produces a "higher principle," but he denies that this series constitutes "progress." Hegel quite specifically rejects any version of evolution of higher species from lower species over time—even going so far as to claim that fossil remains were "paintings."[37] Faced with the overwhelming acceptance of evolution in biology today, I believe—contrary to Findlay—that Hegel would admit its empirical truth but question its ideological foundations. The basic issue finally is not whether there is some relation in time between higher and lower forms but what the theoretical concept is for this process, and here I believe Hegel would stick firmly to a difference between natural evolution and historical progress.

Any characterization of the difference between a scale of nature (or evolution) and true history involves Hegel's technical notion of "the Negative," which can be understood in the quotation above by his use of the persistent contrast between "internal" and "external" relations. In nature or natural evolution the negative is not a true principle because the existence of one form makes no internal comment on another. To be sure, natural species fight and are in constant external relations to one another, but the existence of one form does not involve the negation of another except through the mediation of the environment. Just as a certain form, it is indifferent to the existence of other forms. This relation, Hegel maintains, is not so in the field of history. Forms of government, styles of art, patterns of culture stand in a relation of internal negation to one another. One cannot be a democrat and a supporter of tyranny, an impressionist and a cubist—to adopt one stance is explicitly or implicitly to negate the other possibility. History is a field of human possibilities to which I may be related either positively or negatively—this is the root of our belief that knowledge of history is practically useful. If this power of "the Negative" were not at work in the area of history, then we could regard it with the theoretical interest which we grant to studies of evolution but not with the practical interest that is so closely tied to historical studies.

Evolution is a theory in natural science, and as such its basic conceptual structure is unsuitable to the study of history and vice versa. Despite the abundant use of biological terminology in historical writing, for example, on the evolution of the British parliament, Hegel would have to regard these notions as mere metaphors at best. He says:

[Natural] development proceeds in an immediate, unopposed,

> unhindered manner. . . . But Spirit is opposed to itself; it has to
> overcome itself as the true hostile obstruction to its aims:
> development, which as such is a calm bringing forth . . . is in
> the Spirit . . . a hard unending battle against itself.[38]

To be sure, evolution is the story of mightly struggles and prodigal
waste of species and individuals in a search for biological stability,
but from Hegel's view it is fundamentally unhindered and unopposed since the various species fall outside one another as forms and
are only externally related. The fact that a certain animal exists in
an environment may threaten the fact of another's existence, but in
the struggles that mark the evolution of parliament we suppose
(sometimes at least) that we do not have merely a struggle for
survival between factions but a struggle over rights. History is a
struggle of cultural individuals asserting a right to exist in virtue of
certain values which essentially negate the values of other cultures.
Cultural choices are regarded by Hegel as exclusionary, and history
is a story of cultural choices. It is this internal exclusionary principle
which Hegel poetically describes as spirit struggling against itself.

If this notion of the negative characterizing history as a field of
possibilities chosen or rejected is to be more than a logical confusion
on Hegel's part, we must distinguish it from the simple principle of
identity. The principle of identity affirms that a cow is not a horse or
an ostrich, and so forth. There is no "internal" relation, however,
between the state of being a cow and the state of being an ostrich. If
I say that what I have before me is "not an ostrich," "not a tea
kettle," "not a dwarf star," I can continue on in an infinite
expansion which will bring me not one step nearer in determining
what it is that I have before me.

Even if I confine my universe of discourse, I can still remain with
external relations. Thus, one cannot be both a single-celled and a
multi-celled animal simultaneously. In this sense one might say that
human beings have some internal relation to single-celled organisms
back in the evolutionary track but that the relation does not really
display the character of the negative. There is nothing in my
existence as a multi-celled creature which *as such* calls into question
the existence of single-celled animals, and we might well live joyfully
together in a commodious environment—or unhappy circumstance
might cause one-celled to eliminate multi-celled, or vice versa. Not
so in the case of impressionists and cubists who differ fundamentally about the right sort of painting. Happily, impressionists

and cubists did manage to paint simultaneously, but the *idea* of cubism was intended as a rejection of the *idea* of impressionism and thus the movements were in fundamental internal opposition. If Hegel's general logical principle that "all negation is determination" is to operate in the realm of history, it must operate on a different assumption than the empty statement of identity which can apply to things in general. A Wittgensteinian language game is a good example of a framework in which "negation is determination." If I see how to play a game, then I have a finite number of counters related in such a fashion that rejection of one "implies" (in a loose sense) the assertion or determination of another. Ordinary games show this aspect quite clearly. "Not foul" means "fair," "Not a touchdown" means "it was ruled illegal" or "he actually dropped the ball," and so forth. We may not be able to tell precisely from a single denial what is being affirmed, but every denial is set in a framework of specific counter assertions.

History, then, for Hegel can be imagined to be a great game of cultural patterns but so related that the negation of any one has determinate consequences. If I don't play the Chinese patriarchal strategy, then I may pick up the Indian caste defense or the Roman legal ploy. These strategies are so related that the acceptance of any one rules out in various ways the others. If one accepts the notion that history is a field of possibilities for human choice but constructs this field on the model of nature and the principle of identity (the relation between multiple species in nature as displayed in evolution), then history is a field of indefinite possibilities. While this may sound free and attractive, it means that I *learn* nothing by the rejection of any of history's options. I can turn to history as an indefinitely rich compendia of life styles, all of which stand in external relation to one another so that in choosing or rejecting any one I make no comment on the others. This is another way of stating the position called "cultural relativism," in which all cultures are regarded as so many natural forms with their own inviolable integrity. To be sure, history has been studied with this implicit assumption, but the assumption undercuts any deeply practical use of history; more important, cultural relativism is basically ahistorical since it treats cultural forms on a naturalistic model.

4 *Subjective Reason*

Objective and Subjective Reason

In the previous chapter I attempted to sketch the precise notion of "reason in history" in the objective dimension as follows: the generic category we are dealing with is *change*, a series of differing events, a process. History is an example of *rational* change. The notion of rational change is sharply distinguished from mere chance connections on the ground that if a process is rational there is an internal connection between events, not merely an external one. Reason as an internal principle of change in history is then contrasted with the sense in which reason is *in* nature. In the case of natural, organic life, an internal principle of change is present in the ordered replication of the species. But such an internal principle of change would not be appropriate for a comprehension of history. In nature, the individual is only valued in terms of the universal species which is repeated in the many particulars, but history must involve an internal principle of order which is *progressive* (nonrepetitive). This can be restated by saying that historical change involves primarily the *career of an individual*. For history, individuality is not reducible to a function of any general, universal factor. The problem of historical change centers on the function of individuality as such, and this Hegel states as a search for the *final purpose of history*. Lacking an intrinsic final purpose, individuality and historical change would collapse back into the categories of nature and accident. I have not attempted to defend the notion of objective reason at all points beyond a mere prima facie plausibility. It would be improper to offer a final defense at this stage since one cannot understand fully why Hegel wants to make these claims about the objective process of history until one examines the subjective sense of reason in history, to which we now turn.

"Subjective" is a term of complex use in Hegel. Sometimes it is used pejoratively to dismiss an opinion as merely idiosyncratic or personal whim. "Subjective" in the sense that I use "subjective reason," however, means "belonging to a thinking subject." In contrast with the doctrine of objective reason, which located reason in a context of "objective," "out-there" processes like accidental and natural causes, subjective reason points to a range of usage which pairs reason with certain mental faculties. The subjective sense of reason is probably more common; if asked to define reason, most people would begin by categorizing it as a mental capacity of some sort. They would be quite unlikely to categorize it as an objective process which contrasts to the workings of nature. Having located reason as a mental capacity, however, there is scarcely any clear cut agreement about what constitutes true rationality and even whether reason is revelatory or harmful. Reason has recently come under attack, in a fashion not dissimilar to the attacks on reason familiar to Hegel, as sterile and abstractive, a force of death, not of life. Hegel's discussion of reason in its subjective range is complex, but it is continuous with a considerable philosophical tradition, most notably Kant's treatment of the dialectic of pure reason in the *Critique of Pure Reason.* In fact, it is in Kant that one finds the distinction between understanding and reason which is critical in comprehending Hegel's views. A full account of reason in Hegel could be as vast as his philosophy, but we can give a fairly clear insight into his views by examining reason as it contrasts to the mental "capacities" of understanding, sense perception, and desire.

Understanding and History: The Universal

In the previous chapter we concentrated on Section A in Hoffmeister's German edition of *Reason in History* which is entitled "Its [world philosophical history's] general concept." It is this section which begins with the magnification of reason as the lord of the world. We traced through the implicit and explicit exposition of objective reason offered there. This same section contains (particularly in Hoffmeister's edition) a sketch of the notion of reason in its subjective range. Hegel's general view of the reciprocity of objective and subjective reason is summed up in the famous epigram which occurs toward the beginning of Section A: "To him who looks at the world rationally, the world looks rationally back."[1]

Having made this remark, he notes that if one looks at the world only from the standpoint of "subjectivity" then he obviously won't find anything "rational" in it. This distinction is not specifically analyzed, but it is easily understood from the subsequent argument. His notion is a common one about the consequences of taking a subjective point of view. We suppose that a subjective point of view precludes "objectivity" or any *universal* truth. We contrast "rational point of view," on the grounds of "objectivity," with the subjective stance. Hegel makes these contrasts,[2] and he insists that his study must proceed from a universal point of view: "But this universal is the infinitely concrete which contains all in itself, which is everywhere actually present."[3] If one had followed the argument on the basis of the normal contrast between the subjective on the one hand and reason as a "universal," "objective" point of view on the other, this remark signals that something more is involved in the notion of reason in history than our usual notions of objectivity or universality. The universal as the *infinitely concrete* is a peculiar Hegelian notion which is central to an understanding of "the rational point of view." He turns directly from this remark about the concrete universal to a comment about the mental faculty he calls "the Understanding."

> History must generally be investigated by means of the Understanding [*Verstand*]; we must conceptually grasp cause and effect. In this manner we will observe the essential in history and disregard what is unessential. The Understanding calls attention to what is important and significant in itself. The Understanding determines what is essential and unessential according to the aim which it is following in the treatment of history. These aims can be of the greatest variety. Once an aim is posited other considerations arise; these are primary and secondary aims. If we compare the historical data with the aims of the Spirit we will have to renounce all that might otherwise be taken for interesting and essential. A content presents itself to Reason which is simply not on the same line as what [merely] happened.[4]

This reference to "the Understanding" is the only unambiguous technical reference to this mental faculty in Hegel's work on philosophy of history. A reader familiar with Hegel's other works from the *Phenomenology* through the *Encyclopedia*, however, would recognize how important this distinction between understanding and reason is in his system. The drawing of such a distinction is not common currency in contemporary thought, and one of the fundamental sources of misreading Hegel is the assumption that when he talks about reason in history he is giving us a doctrine which *he* would have regarded as an account of understanding in history. Despite the lack of explicit reference to the understanding in *Reason in History*, it is essential that we realize that the doctrine of *reason* in history is implicitly set against what he is rejecting: a doctrine of understanding in history. Many of his criticisms of other kinds of history, for example, critical history, formalist history, seem to be based on the judgment that they use understanding in investigating history rather than the categories of reason.

Findlay gives a good brief characterization of the understanding:

> The kind of thought characteristic of a formal deductive system is called by Hegel the thought of the Understanding, a thought characterized by great fixity and definiteness of notions, presuppositions and deductive procedures, as well as by an extreme stress on the distinctness and independence of one notion or principle from another.[5]

Correlative with this "definiteness" of the notions utilized by the understanding is their abstractness. The understanding in Kant's philosophy is the product of the application of transcendental logic to the matter of sensation. In Hegel's view, this is the application of abstract universal concepts to the actual given, the application of laws to instances.[6] The material of sensation, the concrete object, is subsumed under an abstract category, the particular is regarded as an instance of a law, nothing more and nothing less. The existential object is quite irrelevant since its being is wholly taken up in the universal form which it instances. This tendency of the understanding is seen with particular clarity in mathematics, where the actual existence of an instance of a mathematical triangle is regarded as irrelevant. But this abstraction is also at work in the natural sciences since when species is regarded as the real, the individual is regarded only as a specimen. It is this static, repetitive view of things which history transcends, going beyond the merely universal to the individual or "the infinitely concrete." The understanding must give way to reason for the comprehension of historical reality.

If the method of understanding is essentially a mathematical method, then it certainly seems that mathematical science is an inadequate model for history. Mathematicians obviously have no interest in the actual existence of the entities they study; they are the very models of a priori reasoners. If history is anything, it certainly deals with existents, and we believe that it is the least a priori of all subjects. Hegel believes that mathematical models subtly invade areas far removed from normal mathematical subject matter so that there are ways of investigating ethics or philosophy *more geometrico*. Such studies are dominated by the basic principle of the understanding which reduces the individual to the universal concept.

There is a passage in which Hegel gives an example of the errors of abstract categories in history, and it seems that the basis of the criticism lies in the resort to the categories of the understanding. He leads into his criticism by referring again to *Verstand*. The German text is somewhat ambiguous about whether *Verstand* is being used in a technical sense or not. Hartman takes it in a nontechnical sense while Sibree regards it as clearly technical, even italicizing "understanding" in one place where there is no such indication in the Karl Hegel text. In this instance I think Sibree is nearer the truth, and I offer his translation. Hegel is discussing the indictment against philosophy which accuses it of insinuating ideas into the empirical data of history and thus not understanding such sciences:

> It must, indeed, allow that it has not that kind of Understanding which is the prevailing one in the domain of those sciences, that it does not proceed according to the categories of such Understanding, but according to the categories of Reason—though at the same time recognizing that Understanding and its true value and position. It must be observed that in this very process of scientific *Understanding*, it is of importance that the essential should be distinguished and brought into relief in contrast with the so-called non-essential.[7]

I am inclined to think that Hegel is alluding to the technical sense of understanding here because of the terminology "categories of Reason" and because he makes the same point in this passage as in the previous passage which clearly *does* employ understanding technically—the point that reason finally determines what is "essential" in history. The example which illustrates the claim of this passage suggests that it is understanding vs. reason which is at issue.

> A similar [inadequate] mode of reasoning is used when it is rightly said that genius, talents, piety, moral virtues and sentiments appear in all zones, under all constitutions, and political conditions. There is no lack of examples to confirm this. There is,

however, this distinction which is derived from the self-consciousness of freedom, that if one wanted to hold that these characteristics were unimportant or unessential, then reflection stops at abstract categories and denies determinate content—for which, it is true, no principle can be supplied by these categories. The viewpoint which adopts such merely formal perspectives presents a vast field of ingenious questions, erudite views, and striking comparisons, seemingly profound reflections and declamations which can be the more brilliant, the more indefinite their subject is.[8]

Hegel finally calls this attitude "formalism" (*Formalismus*). Formalism is the besetting sin of the understanding because it neglects determinate content. As particular examples of formalist errors he lists the comparison of Homeric poems with Indian epics, comparison of the *Tao* of Chinese philosophy with the One of the Eleatics and Spinoza, and he concludes:

> [The formalist ideas] are products of a reflective thinking which in its universalizing is more fertile in abstracting and naming essential distinctions without going into the true depth of the matter. This is general *culture*—something merely formal which aims at nothing more than the analysis of a subject, whatever it may be, into its constituent elements and the comprehension of these elements through conceptual definitions and forms of thought.[9]

What exactly is the error of "formalism," or of the understanding, in historical thinking? The section in which these passages are contained is concerned with "Peoples," who are for Hegel the true individuals of history. The error of formalism is that, since it proceeds by abstraction, it regards something like "moral virtue" as a common topic in the lives of pagans and Christians, while Hegel wishes to insist that the individual spirit of the people gives a determinate content to moral virtue which makes cross-cultural comparisons superficial and unhistorical. Formalism under the aegis of the understanding does single out what is "essential" insofar as it organizes the mass of facts into certain determinate conceptions which are indeed essential and important aspects of the life of a people. But the understanding neglects the fact that we are dealing with historical subject matter and that these universal categories, as such, turn out to be *inessential* because for history the determinate content of something like a moral system affects the very notion of morality itself. As quoted before: "There is not only classical form but also classical content."[10]

An almost exact analogy of this Hegelian criticism of "formalism" in history can be found in various modern criticism of "formalist" theories of art where the same point is made—that formalists neglect "determinate content." Arnold Isenberg has written a persuasive refutation of formalism in art which makes the crucial point which Hegel is using in his analysis of historical thinking.[11] Isenberg says that the impetus of formalism comes from a realization that one cannot evaluate works of art simply in terms of their subject matter. There have been as many bad religious paintings or landscapes as good, so the proclaimed subject cannot determine our aesthetic evaluation. This led the formalists to insist that what was essential in painting was not the subject matter but the formal elements—line, color, organization, and so forth. Surely there is something correct about this notion. It is the handling of material, the formal organization which is essential in evaluating painting, not its subject matter as such. But, says Isenberg, the formalists are seriously mistaken if they think that their new language of shape and color comes any closer to describing the essential characteristics of a painting than the old language of subject matter.

> [A]ppreciative criticism is subject inevitably to this limitation, that while form is individual and determinate, language is general and (in W. E. Johnson's sense) merely determinable. "In composition," wrote Emerson, "the What is of no importance compared to the How." But How is nothing but the determinate *What*. The language of subject-matter cannot express the How because it touches upon only those characteristics of the form that it shares with certain whole classes of forms. A swerve in the outline, the slightest variation in the shading of a head represents the gulf between the master and the dub, but no ready distinction of language corresponds to it. *Formalism* strives to repair this deficiency with the help of an explicit sensory vocabulary—"line," "plane," "color," "light" and their derivatives.... But the language of formalism, we must observe, is itself general and determinable.... It is still necessary to look at the picture—we could not construct it from the [formalist] description.[12]

I have very little notion of what a picture is like if I simply know the title: *Death of Acteon*. What do I know if I am told that the painting is an organization of warm colors, heavy impasto arranged in a pyramidal shape? Something, no doubt, but I finally know what these words mean only in the presence of the actual work of art. The language of formalism is just as abstract and general as the old language of subject matter. The shape of the painting is a certain determinate line and cannot be adequately characterized by the most precise formal categories. Titian's *Death of Acteon* is an organization of shapes, colors, and lines, but, as Isenberg remarks, for all that I cannot really look at it as if it were a Kandinsky because these shapes and colors are the shapes of bodies and bushes—not any bodies, but these quite determinate Titianesque bodies.

In Isenberg's account, then, we have an inversion of essential/inessential similar to that which Hegel alleges is the case in historical thinking. In ordinary scientific understanding, when I seize the essence I seize the universal and ignore the concrete particular. Waiting at the traffic light, I ask my companion, "What color is it?" I expect to be told it is either red or green. I would be amazed and annoyed if told, "A curious, dull sheen, highlighted by small moving reflections from darting headlamps, a rippling pattern of light on a ground somewhere between dirty cerise and mauve." That kind of talk directs me to the determinate content, while I am interested only in a definite abstract quality. Directing attention to determinate content is a fundamental shift in perspective and must not be confused with a simple change of direction for the understanding. There may be an infinity of abstract qualities serving an equal number of interests—a traffic engineer may well be interested in color and reflection not of *this* lamp as such but in terms of certain general problems about traffic signals. The aesthetic shift is a shift away from looking for abstract qualities at all to an appreciation of the determinate form.

Another way of characterizing this shift is to note that, for the understanding, language can be descriptive while, for the art critic as Isenberg comprehends his function, language is hermeneutic. We accept that "green" is descriptive in the case of the signal lamp when we are interested only in the general notion of the color. Language which is general and only determinable is accepted as describing, when all we are interested in is the abstract quality instanced in the presented object. In the case of the object of art, however, no critical "description" can finally tell us what the picture actually looked like. We simply cannot know the exact character of Greek wall-paintings since they have all been destroyed; even if we had detailed descriptions, they would remain empty. In hermeneutic discourse the immediate experience of the object must be the final interpretation for the language.

If we return to Hegel's criticism of historical formalism, the application of the principles developed in the discussion of artistic formalism can be applied. Our interest in history moves to the individual, not to the universal. It is true that the Greeks and the Christians both have religions in their cultures and that these religions are extremely important in their societies. To discover this much is the work of understanding, but the understanding falters at this point and assumes that the universal concept "religion" remains the same while admitting of different contents—the Greeks believed in many gods, the Christians in only one. Hegel wants to say, on the contrary, that while both cultures may be said to have a "religion" the determinate content of these two "religions" makes it doubtful whether they are really the same kind of cultural phenomenon. We would say that the whole "spirit" of the two enterprises is different despite a topical similarity. The understanding brushes over these differences as *mere* matters of content and declares that the form, "religion," is a constant, comprehensible category in various cultures.

Hegel's attack on formalism and reliance on the understanding offers a basis for comprehending his repeated claims that his philosophy of history is truly empirical, while it is critical and formalist historians who are a priorist:

> We have to take history as it is; we have to proceed historically, empirically (*historisch, empirisch*). Among other things we must not be distracted by the specialist historians; for at least among German historians, even those who possess the greatest authority and who indulge themselves in so-called *Quellenstudien*, do what they accuse the philosopher of doing, that is making *a priori* fictions in history (*apriorische Erdichtungen*).[13]

These claims of empiricism and attacks on the "critical historians" who practice *Quellenstudien* are among the most puzzling and embarrassing claims in Hegel's philosophy of history. He enjoys little reputation as an empiricist, and he seems to be attacking just those figures who significantly advanced the scientific study of history in the nineteenth century. Let us take up the problem of empiricism first.

The Hempelian theory which we have discussed in the previous chapter is widely regarded as an empirical theory—it certainly is by its supporters. It is sometimes alleged that the historian who writes conventional history without explicit reference to explanatory laws is a mere armchair narrator who lacks a proper respect for the validation of his claims. The historian is urged by the Hempelian model to make explicit the explanatory laws to which he appeals, so that they can be adequately tested in proper empirical disciplines like economics or sociology. Even historians who may never have heard of Hempel's theory by name have been affected by the contention within the historical profession that historians should rely more heavily on the social sciences to justify their conclusions. From Hegel's standpoint, however, the Hempelian theory of explanation by laws is not at all empirical; it is essentially a priori, the exercise of the understanding.

In the *Phenomenology*, Hegel discusses at some length the concepts of "explanation" and "law" as they operate in science. This discussion constitutes a major part of his treatment of the understanding, and it is not surprising that a theory like Hempel's—*because* of its reliance on explanation and laws—fails to provide an appropriate model for historical thought. Before briefly sketching Hegel's strictures on explanatory laws, one can point out in general why he regards such theories as nonempirical. Hempel's theory is a modern version of formalism. Insofar as it searches for *laws* of events, it must regard events as properly universalizable. If one wants to explain the Russian Revolution on the basis of a general theory about revolutions, then one must assume that there have been many "revolutions" on the basis of which empirical generalizations can be drawn. One moves then to an induction of past revolutions, American, French, Chinese, and so on, but Hegel objects at once. The sense in which these many revolutions form a common class is only formalistic; once one goes beyond the merest sketch, the determinate content of these revolutions should make it clear that this universal categorization fails to illuminate what really interests us, their *historical* character. As our discussion of art and the formalist mistake showed, the meaning of the universal can only be made plain in the presence of the actual individual item. The Russian Revolution is not finally made comprehensible by a general theory of revolutions as much as by a direct assessment of the empirical data as an individual, nonrepeatable, novel event. From this standpoint, there is considerable validity to Hegel's claim that he is truly empirical since, unlike the formalist historian, he does not treat the concrete individuals of history as mere instances of formal types. As in the case of art, one has to "directly experience" the proper object.

Hegel's treatment of explanation and law in the *Phenomenology* is not much clearer than most of that volume, but he appears to be making a specific point against *any* general theory of "knowledge" by means of explanatory laws, a point which resembles contemporary criticism of Hempel's theory of historical explanation. For this reason it is worth attempting an explication of the central passage from the *Phenomenology* on explanation.

> This kingdom of laws is indeed the truth for Understanding; and that truth finds its content in the distinction which lies in the law. At the same time, however, this kingdom of laws...does not give all the fullness of the world of appearance. The law is present therein, but is not all the appearance present; under ever-varying circumstances the law has an ever-varying actual existence.... This defect in the law has to be brought out in the law itself. What seems defective in it is that while it no doubt has difference within it, it contains this in a merely universal indeterminate way. So far, however, as it is not *law* in general, but *a* law, it has determinateness within it; and as a result there are found an indeterminate plurality of laws. But this plurality is rather itself a defect; it contradicts the principle of understanding.... It must, therefore, let the many laws coalesce into a single law.... [But] when the laws thus coincide...they lose their specific character. The law becomes more and more abstract and superficial.[14]

The message of this passage is not immediately clear, but I believe it can be translated into more modern and comprehensible form. The notion of laws and explanations rests on a background distinction between laws and *instances* of laws. We say that the radiator cracking is an instance of a certain set of laws operating under certain initial conditions. Hegel calls this the distinction between laws and appearance, that is, the phenomenon *in* which the law appears as an instance. This distinction is crucial since it is the appearance that the law is supposed to explain. But, of course, the instance is an instance *of* the law, otherwise the law would not apply. What is there, then, that retains the character of appearance; how is the instance seen *as* instance if its entire intelligible character is a mere instance of the law? In the case of mathematics, the instance vanishes to nothing, and I regard the intelligible form as the only real aspect of the situation. Something like this vanishing of the instance into pure universal form is the dream of the understanding in the natural sciences. But obviously it is more complicated than that in nature. Mathematical objects (instances even) are much more clear, separate, and distinct than radiators. Radiators stand at the intersection of all sorts of laws: physical, chemical, meteorological, sociological, and so on. Thus, the instance of this radiator cracking is very difficult to capture under a proper set of laws since the major premise stating the laws will be incredibly long.

The person offering general laws as explanation always notes that there are all kinds of parameters that it would be extremely difficult to include, and so he contents himself with the principle laws for the phenomenon and relegates the remaining possible laws to "etc." Hempel himself has abandoned the pure deductive model in favor of "explanation sketches" to point out that one never can give the full, ironclad deduction which the explanation by law model suggests. The "etc" character of explanations by law—the incompleteness which suggests explanation *sketches* rather than explanations—is what Hegel seems to be referring to when he speaks about the fact that in explaining the "ever-varying circumstances the law has an ever-varying actual existence." That is, *the* explanation for *this* instance may be quite different from *the* explanation for some other instance which at first appears to be just the same. Because of the "ever-varying" circumstances, there is no guarantee that the explanation of two instances of a radiator cracking will be the same. The lack of unity of the explanation is "disguised" in the indeterminateness of the statement of laws, covered by "etc" added to what are regarded as the principal laws in effect. The "etc" indicates the possible difference between two seemingly identical explanations of the seemingly same event but as Hegel says it contains this "in a merely universal indeterminate way."

Hegel then goes on to suggest that if one were to try to sketch out this indeterminate conglomerate of laws contained in the "etc" statement one would arrive at laws which become "more and more abstract and superficial." He illustrates this—not very clearly—by sketching out the law of universal gravitation and ends by saying: "In contrast, then, with determinate law stands universal attraction, or the bare conception of law."[15] The line of argument here is similar, in my judgment, to criticism actually brought against the

Hempelian theory. Thus Alan Donagan cites as a putative historical law— "You cannot, without increasing productivity, raise the real income of the working population"—and says:

> [This] is simply false, as ancient Rome showed by living on tribute; but if you modify it to, "If the real income of the working population is to be raised, assuming full employment, that no new natural resources are discovered and that income cannot be obtained from outside, e.g., by begging, borrowing or stealing, then productivity must be increased," you reduce it to an application of the law of the conservation of energy.[16]

The criticism seems to follow Hegel's line quite well. One states the general law, but immediately one can think of cases in which it would be falsified (the ever-varying conditions), and, instead of abandoning the explanation, one tries to fix it up by adding further conditions. What is produced, finally, is a statement which turns out to be extremely abstract and superficial, quite remote from the seeming problem of accounting for an increase in wealth. Donagan identifies this expanded statement with the principle of the conservation of energy and says that since it is a physical law it obviously won't do for history. For Hegel the argument cuts even deeper. Hegel suggests that finally the argument reduces to "the bare conception of law." The principle of the conservation of energy is a curious *physical* law since it appears to say merely that causality applies—you cannot get something out of nothing in any system. It is more the "bare conception of law" since it states that there must be a causal explanation for the effect; energy is merely transferred in a system, not created. What emerges at last from the expanded statement about productivity and prosperity is that added wealth must come from somewhere, a new effect must have a cause. But that gives us no information at all about the causes of this increase in wealth.

Hegel sums up his critique of the understanding and its attempt to offer explanation by laws by saying that what begins as a determinate explanation is, by reason of its failure actually to reach *this* appearance, expanded in more and more indeterminate ways until what is finally left as an "explanation" is not at all determinate (directed at the particular instance at hand) but a mere allegiance to explanation in general. What at first appears to be strict empirical explanation by means of a determinate empirical law turns out to be mere a priorism, the statement that the effect must have a cause.

What lies at the base of this failure of the understanding, the notion of explanation by law or formalist history, is the inability to take the *instance* seriously. In mathematics, the true domain of the understanding, the instance does vanish wholly into the intelligible form. In natural science one may, perhaps, approximate to this mathematical treatment of actual physical objects. (Hegel and Aristotle seem to be two philosophers who reject the notion of a mathematical physics because physical objects cannot be treated as mere intelligibles.) However one decides on the role of mathematical method in nature, for history this neglect of the instance, the turning of the individual object into a universal form, is unhistorical and unempirical.

If we turn from the criticism of formalist history to Hegel's strictures on the "critical historians," we can discern one of the problems that Hegel has to solve if he wishes to offer a view of history which in some way parallels the account given about art appreciation. In that account, following Isenberg, we insisted that formalist critics were wrong in their theories of art because they assumed that formalist language was closer to the essence of the art object than the older language of subject matter. But no language really is adequate *except in the actual presence of the object*. The art object is uniquely individual, and one comes to understand the critical language via the direct appreciation of the actual concrete instance. Critical language is parasitic on the art object and it becomes empty when the object disappears. One of the obvious problems with this model for history is to identify the analogue in the historical case of direct acquaintance with the art object. Isn't the problem of history precisely the fact that the actual individuals, the states and peoples of the past, no longer exist? We have to guess at their character from accounts much in the manner that we have to guess at the character of Zeuxis's paintings from descriptions—a hopeless task. A skeptical attitude about knowing the real past obviously can be derived from applying something like the art model to history and then deciding that the historian has an impossible job since his object is either wholly vanished or exists only in fragments.

This leads us to the problem of the critical historians. As noted, Hegel seems to take a continuously antipathetic attitude toward *Quellenstudien*. He accuses historians who practice these critical methods of being the real a priorists. In part, this criticism is based on faults which *Quellenstudien* share with formalist historians. I am far from being an expert on the history of historiography, but even a superficial acquaintance with *Quellenstudien* would indicate that some criticism of source material was not in the direction of finding the actual historical fact as much as it was a reduction of the sources to some general anthropological theory. Having assumed on the basis of some general theory—often derived from general theories about language—what the normative state of primitive society must have been, the critical historian proceeded to show the falsity of source documents to the abstract model. But there is a particular problem in connection with critical history that would trouble Hegel and may account for his hostility. Since the critical historian studies sources, he often deals with those historians whom Hegel labels "original historians." They are the contemporary witnesses whom the latter-day historian calls into question. Hegel does not seem opposed to a critical analysis of sources as such—his comments on Niebuhr and Livy are pertinent to this point. What he must oppose is the complete critical evaporation of original history.

A critical historian by definition says that the report he has before him is subject to critical evaluation as to its truth. As far as original historians are concerned, this statement is subject to considerable limitation. The original historian must somehow directly embody the spirit of his age. Thucydides' speeches, as we have them, may not be the actual words but they reflect the times and the spirit of the people. By what standard will the latter-day critical historian find falsity in the original historian? If, as we suggested above, he criticizes the actual report of the original historian in terms of some favored general model, then what emerges will be something which fails to reflect the individual spirit of a people, which is precisely where the value of the original historian lies. If the critical historian simply does critical studies and shows the biases and partialities of the original historian, this can be valuable, as Hegel says, but one can't pass this off as history itself. Why? Because history finally is organized around the presentation of a people and its spirit. For this presentation we must *fundamentally* validate the work of the original historian since he is the primary source of the self-reflected-ness which constitutes the spirit of a people—he *is* the spirit of the people in its immediate reflectiveness. Insofar as critical history involves a *total* questioning of sources it would be precluded from constructing history, since any historian must accept some original history as the true embodiment of a spirit even if it also contains "false" descriptions. It is original history, then, which must be the Hegelian analogue for the art object in our discussion of the errors of formalism. Original history is the direct, immediate presentation of the spirit of a people on the basis of which all latter-day "critical" studies must rest if they are to remain proper history at all.

This analogy between the presentation of the art object and the role of original history may appear somewhat strained. After all, the art object is empirically given, in no uncertain sense of "empirical," and it seems odd to say that Thucydides' history is an equivalent "empirical" presentation of Greece during the Peloponnesian War. Perhaps one can gather some distant sense in which Hegel views his theory of history as properly empirical, contrary to the formalists, from his insistence on "the individual" as against the "universal." Still, the art example and our normal expectations lead us to think of "empirical" as associated with something like direct sensory perception, and that seems to be impossible in history except in the odd way in which original historians "directly present" the spirit of their age. What is needed is some further discussion of individuality as a category. We can proceed on that road by turning to Hegel's views about sense perception and its ability to grasp "the individual."

History and Sense Perception: The Particular

Hegel insists that he will proceed "empirically" in his investigation of history, but he also claims that it is reason which is the sole key to the comprehension of history. How can the two claims be reconciled? How can the man who says "To him who looks at the world rationally, the world looks rationally back" turn right around and say that he is looking at his subject matter empirically? Most contemporary philosophers regard rationalism and empiricism as contradictory schools of philosophy, and they neatly divide the history of philosophy between the continental rationalists—Descartes, Spinoza, and Leibniz—and the British empiricists—Locke, Berkeley, and Hume. Kant somehow tries to overcome this dichotomy, but Hegel is the super-rationalist of them all, as certainly seems to be borne out by the great initial quotation from *Reason in History*.

In the previous section it was necessary to delve into Hegel's general system to distinguish reason from understanding. In this section we shall take the same tack in attempting to come to closer grips with his "empiricism." I can easily imagine a contemporary philosopher or historian agreeing with the strictures made on the understanding in the previous section, on the ground that in some sense history is concerned with the individual occurrence rather than with the general form. One could evaluate this interest in individual occurrence as the glory of history (as Hegel obviously does) or as an example of its intellectual poverty (the historian as mere mechanic applying the great general laws to particular cases and failing to come up to the true stance of a scientist). Nevertheless, no one that I am aware of is willing to see history totally absorbed into sociology: poor or rich, history is interested in the individual case. We have already suggested that insofar as one is interested in individual instances, there is a tendency toward empiricism because the individual instance, it is generally assumed, can only be given in direct empirical awareness. Thus, a contemporary thinker following the argument against the understanding might well assume that what Hegel was really interested in was the rights of empiricism rather than the role of reason. More specifically, there would be a strong presumption to see the polemic against understanding as establishing the role of sense perception in history since it is widely thought that sense perception presents the actual, individual case to our awareness. Instead of "Reason in History," why don't we have a treatise on "Sense Perception in History"? That would seem closer to the truth of the matter if one insists on history as particularly concerned with individuality.

The line of reasoning which would locate "individuality" as the proper object of sense perception, or which would argue that it is only through sense perception that one makes contact with individual cases, is one which Hegel considers very explicitly and rejects at the beginning of the *Phenomenology of the Spirit*. We can approach Hegel's views through a classic modern formulation of the problem of universal and "individual"; this approach will be useful because it not only will help to clarify Hegel's eventual argument but also because the formulation is widely shared and can be pointed to as the basis for misinterpretation of Hegel.

A distinction seemingly very similar to Hegel's division of universal and individual has received a classical formulation in Bertrand Russell's distinction between knowledge by description and knowledge by acquaintance. Knowledge by description is very much akin to knowledge of universals. A sentence like "The cat is on the mat" is an example of knowledge by description. If true, it describes some fact and hence yields knowledge. The "fact" which it describes, however, is one about universals. What the sentence says in effect is that an instance of the species "cat" bears a certain universally characterizable relation ("being on") to some other instance of a universal, "mat-ness." Russell is quite clear that what is described in such ordinary sentences is *not* the uniquely individual situtation. Only "basic propositions" relate to the immediately given as such. No examples can be given of basic propositions since all propositions formulated from normal words go beyond the data immediately present. The stock notion is that a basic proposition is "stated" in a kind of indicating gesture: "there is this." Russell even proposed a theory of "logically proper names" (words like "this") whose prime function was to direct the listener to the actual given.

This Russellian distinction has reasonably wide acceptance among philosophers, though there are many who reject Russell's development of the doctrine. There is a fair agreement that there is some distinction to be made between knowledge of universals and knowledge of particulars—the "this's" of the world. It might seem then that Hegel's insistence on the importance of the actual empirical individual for historical knowing was a precursor of the modern notion of knowledge by acquaintance. There are, however, many problems about any such identification. Not the least of the problems is that almost everyone is agreed that knowledge of particulars is "unspeakable." In the *Lectures on Logical Atomism* there is a very amusing exchange between Russell and a questioner.[17] Russell points out that it is very difficult to speak a basic proposition because by the time you utter the phrase the direct experience which it is supposed to indicate has gone by. When someone from the audience picked him up on this difficulty, the best that he could offer was that one should speak as quickly as possible. If historical knowing was equivalent to knowledge by acquaintance, not only would we be hard pressed to have *acquaintance* with the past but even if we had such acquaintance we would have no words to describe what was seen, we could only gesture. To the extent that one wishes to call attention to the radical particularity of things, one is left without any workable language since language is measured to the universal, not the particular; one is left pointing and uttering "this."

One could easily confuse the claims put forth in the previous section for the centrality of the individual (in art and history) and the "hermeneutic function" of discourse (in art and history) with the centrality of particularity and the indicative function of language in Russell's theory, but the results would be devastating for any sensible notion of historical knowledge. In Hegel there is a triple distinction where Russell only offers two choices. In his "doctrine of the Notion," Hegel distinguishes three moments: universality, specificity and individuality. The first two distinctions roughly parallel Russell's knowledge by description (universals) and knowledge by acquaintance (particulars), and Hegel is very concerned to make sure that his third category, the individual, is confused with neither of the other categories. The individual is, in fact, the dialectical synthesis of particularity and universality. Thus Kojève states the outcome of the struggle of particular and universal: "In its perfection, the idea reveals itself through the idea of *Individuality*—that is, of satisfaction of the real or active synthesis of the *particularist* and *universalist* tendencies of human existence."[18]

The fundamental confusion involved in false empiricisms in history is the failure to see the difference between particulars and individuals. Sense perception gives us contact with particulars, and at first sight this appears the real, rich content of knowledge. But Hegel criticizes the value of sense perception in a manner which seems quite appropriate when one considers Russell's troubles with "knowledge by acquaintance." This is Findlay's summation of the argument:

> Hegel begins [his account of knowledge] by dealing with Sense-certainty, the state of mind in which, in Russellian terms, we enjoy a direct acquaintance with some object, which we *app*rehend without seeking to *com*prehend or describe. The content of such sensuous apprehension seems to common thought indefinitely rich—all comprehension seems merely to select from it and abridge it—it also seems to be the most solidly true element of our knowledge, all other knowledge being based upon it.... Hegel maintains, however, that such Sense-certainty is the most emptily abstract of consciousness: its whole content can be covered by such bald phrases as "There is this" or simply "It is." To say something *more* about what confronts us in Sense-awareness is at once to pass beyond it, to dissolve it into a series of concepts or universals, with which step the solidity of our knowledge will at once suffer an attenuation.[19]

We are thus faced with a dilemma as far as historical awareness of individuals is concerned: if we seek to locate the individual as the object of sense awareness, we will locate the particular, which, after first seeming to offer the richest and most determinate content, quickly dissolves into only the most bare and abstract knowledge. On the other hand, if we follow the line into the world of concepts and universals, as Findlay says we must, we will eventaully end with the discussion of the understanding and the allegation that attempts to understand individual instances as cases of determinate laws dissolve into bare and abstract assertions of the conception of law. Both universal and particular prove valueless for comprehending the individual. Given only the two choices of empiricism (sense awareness) or rationalism (as the universalizing knowledge of understanding), we cannot locate anything like proper history in either category. History becomes either unspeakably particular or totally absorbed into general law. Hegel, however, is not left with the dichotomous distinction stated by Russell. If we combine some Russellian and Hegelian notions, we can generate the following table:

Form of knowledge	Object	Science	Mental faculty
by description	universals	natural science mathematics	understanding
by acquaintance	particulars	(no communicable knowledge)	sense perception
by hermeneusis	individuals	history	reason

"Knowledge by hermeneusis" is a category I have inserted to parallel the comments previously made about hermeneutic discourse in the arts. The root notion of hermeneusis is that of a form of communicative discourse in the presence of the individual object discussed which illuminates that object while, paradoxically, gaining its final meaning from the direct awareness of the object. It is unlike knowledge by description since, in that form, discourse wholly substitutes for the "object." Since the "object" is a universal character, the generalized nature of language is quite sufficient to capture its reality. Hermeneusis differs from "knowledge by acquaintance" in that, while they both depend on the presence of the object for meaningfulness, hermeneusis is not a mere indicative gesture at the indeterminate; it is an ordered and intelligible discourse which leads the hearer on to "appreciate" the object in its very individuality. No doubt one might wonder how the trick is carried off and whether any speech can be genuinely hermeneutic, but for now it seems sufficient to say that art critics do seem to do it. It may be even more puzzling to think of primary historical discourse as "hermeneutic," but insofar as historical discourse must convey the spirit of something individual in articulate form, it seems to have some strong resemblance to "knowledge by hermeneusis." Finally, one might think that this new category was an interesting addition but wonder whether Hegel ever thought of any such curious way of knowing. It seems to me most plausible that phenomenology is just such a hermeneutic endeavor. I will not argue the point here except to note that the famous convolutions of the Preface to the *Phenomenology* suggest the stance of a man attempting to articulate that which is already fully in view.

So far I have merely stated Hegel's views on the "cognitive" awareness which is necessary for history. I have pointed out his curious combination of the empirical and the rational in historical awareness and tried to exorcise two of the most common confusions that can occur in trying to interpret Hegel's views: the confusion of reason with understanding and the confusion of his empiricism with empiricisms of sense perception. I have not attempted to prove the *necessity* of generating any mental capacities beyond the understanding and sense perception—categories which, one should reiterate, seem to be quite sufficient to many distinguished philosophers both past and present. All I can say at this point is that, if one wishes to construct a view of historical awareness which seems to fit with our common intuition that history is an *intelligible* study of individuals, neither understanding or sense perception will suffice. Insofar as this is a commentary on *Reason in History* and not the *Phenomenology*, I am content to leave the matter at that point. It is the function of the earlier work to "deduce" the necessity of reason and history for any proper view of reality. I will assume that the reader of this commentary is not prepared to jettison historical awareness totally, so that my task is simply to show how Hegel believes it is possible—and that by the faculty of reason.

Self-Consciousness, Individuality, and Reason

The concluding sections of the *Phenomenology* dealing with the understanding are among the most extraordinary in the entire volume. By a series of dialectical passes which, as Findlay suggests, are likely to make the reader feel as if he were lost in an Indochinese forest, Hegel changes the entire focus of his inquiry from the cognitive problems of sense perception, understanding, laws, and explanations to ethical and political problems. We move in a few pages from a technical discussion of electricity to the famous passage on "master and slave" which has been of immense political effect as worked out in Marxist thought. The intermediary for this extraordinary shift—which Hegel appears to think follows quite naturally—is a section on "self-consciousness." There is a prima facie plausibility to this linkage if one stops to consider the notion of self-consciousness. On the one hand self-consciousness seems to be a kind of knowledge, a type of consciousness or cognitive awareness, but at the same time *self*-consciousness seems to have very considerable relation to ethical doctrine. Moral notions like personal "integrity" obviously depend on self-knowledge. Self-knowledge is frequently stated as an effective means for changing one's behavior and it is sometimes claimed to be the "moral" goal for which an individual should strive.

Hegel's use of the notion of self-consciousness to bridge a gap in his presentation of spirit is not my primary concern. Self-consciousness however, offers an effective key to explicating the problem of historical consciousness and the role of reason in that consciousness. Self-consciousness, individuality, and reason are intimately related for Hegel and form the core, therefore, of proper historical consciousness. Let us examine, then, what is contained in the notion of self-consciousness. Here is Kojève's account of Hegel's view:

> Now, the analysis of "thought," "reason," "understanding," and so on—in general the cognitive, contemplative, passive behaviour of a being or a knowing subject—never reveals the why or how of the birth of the word "I", and consequently of self-consciousness—that is, of human reality. The man who contemplates is "absorbed" in what he contemplates; the "knowing subject" "loses" himself in the object that is known. Contemplation reveals the object, not the subject. . . . The man who is "absorbed" by the object that he is contemplating can be "brought back to himself" only by a Desire; by the desire to eat, for example.[20]

The "knowing subject" is not a true *self*-consciousness; it is only what Kant called a "Transcendental ego." This is perfectly obvious. When one says "I know the Pythagorean theorem," it is not "I" as named individual that is involved. Russell's knowledge by acquaintance may be person-referential since my own peculiar sense data seem to be the thing known—that is, only I, B. Russell, can perceive them. But in all cases except that queer knowledge—if it should be called knowledge at all—the character of the person as a particular self is not in question. The anonymity and communicability of science are based on the fact that scientific knowledge is not person-referential. Man as knower, then, cannot be the generator of self-consciousness; the positing of a particular, personal center of consciousness must be generated by some other fact about human beings. "[S]elf-consciousness is the state of *Desire* in general."[21]

While desire is the root of self-positing, the factor which transforms man from an angelic intelligence, from a transcendental ego without particularity, into self-consciousness, desire hardly seems appropriate to serve as the fundamental category for historical consciousness. Just as we asked how Hegel could assert the centrality of reason and yet claim to proceed empirically, so we have to ask how this rooting of self-consciousness in desire squares with the role of reason in self-consciousness. After all, desire is something that men share with animals. Do animals have self-consciousness? Do animals have a history? Even if we restrict ourselves to human desires, how can desire generate the individuality which we have indicated is Hegel's particular interest in history? Aren't human desires rather drearily common? Reduce human reality to its desires, and one can quickly iron out the rich variety of cultures into just so many decorations on the basic lusts. Kojève indicates the necessary next step:

> The positive content of the I, constituted by negation, is a
> function of the positive content of the negated non-I. [The
> object of my desire, the nonself which stands over and against
> me.] If, then, the Desire is directed toward a "natural" non-I,
> the I, too, will be "natural". The I created by the active satis-
> faction of such a Desire will have the same nature as the things
> toward which that Desire is directed: it will be a "thingish" I,
> a merely living I, an animal I. And this natural I, a function
> of the natural object, can be revealed to itself and to others
> only as Sentiment of self. It can never attain Self-Consciousness.[22]

Human beings in the expression of basic animal desires do not attain true self-consciousness, only the sentiment of self. Animal desires in man and beast are "natural" desires in the sense that they follow the logic of "nature" which we discussed in the previous chapter. Natural desires are essentially universal and repetitive. They are repetitive in a double sense: first, the animal repeatedly desires more or less the same thing and, second, animal desiring is in effect a return to a state of satiation. The animal moves from being full to being hungry to being full again. Animal desire is universal in the sense that the object of the desire is something generic—I want food or, even more specifically, an ear of corn. Now, I have to eat this particular ear of corn, to be sure, since I can't eat a universal, but the particularity of the ear is of no concern. Any similar ear will do. Human gourmets are often interested in the aesthetic individuality of meals, and they do not eat merely to restore satiety but in a continuous quest of gastronomic excellence—eating can become infected with history.

The character of self-consciousness is wholly determined by the character of the object of desire. If we are seeking self-consciousness as *individual* self-consciousness, then we can see from the previous analysis of nature in chapter 3 that a natural object will fail to yield individual self-consciousness since the character of the *natural* object is wholly taken up in its universal character as a specimen of a generic type. Desire must fasten on a *nonnatural* object if the self-consciousness which it produces is to be individualized. What can qualify as a nonnatural object which, when it becomes the focus of consciousness, yields individuality? An obvious candidate which immediately presents itself in the light of our previous discussion is an object of art. Art objects are by definition nonnatural (at least in an Aristotelian world they are), and, as our discussion from Isenberg indicated, our interest in the art object is for the individual object and the individual style.

"Art object" in any strict sense is not the proper object of historical study for Hegel (though we shall discuss later the way in which history of art parallels much that Hegel thinks is true about history in general), but it is worth spending a moment on this hypothesis before moving to Hegel's more precise formulation. It is true, in some sense, that man as *artificer*, the maker of tools and culture, is the peculiar subject of history. This is a widely held notion, but one must guard against an overall naturalistic framework for this position which would invalidate, in Hegel's view at least, a genuinely historical interest. There are theories of art and culture which are at least as old as the great myth of Protagoras (in

Plato's dialogue by that name) in which man is indeed the artificer but the aim of art is strictly to imitate nature. In Protagoras's myth, the flint ax does for man what the claw and muscle do for the panther. Man accomplishes by tools what animals do by nature. The total situation of the Protagorean theory is finally natural, then, since the end accomplished by art is natural, that is, preservation of life. (It is for this reason, no doubt, that Plato rejects Protagoras's position.) The nonnatural art object is only a means to a natural end and as such it is infected with the disinterest in individuality which we normally have toward natural objects. Tools accomplishing generic ends are treated as mere instances to be discarded as individuals. Part of the shock value of the Pop-art which exalts the soup can, the typewriter, and the electric plug to places in museums is that we no longer read the objects generically but individually, in the manner that we normally read works of fine art.

If desire for a nonnatural object is the basis of individual self-consciousness, then the nonnatural object cannot be seen simply as an artificial tool for accomplishing an end set by nature. This is a somewhat metaphysical way of signifying that a true historical interest cannot be sustained by a theory of human culture which is in the last analysis naturalistic in the Protagorean manner. Human culture is indeed the peculiar interest of historians but only if the basic theory of culture is one which sees culture as accomplishing nonnatural ends.

Objects of fine art, as objects of consciousness, have some of the characteristics which are essential for a proper object of historical consciousness in Hegel. In particular, a common contemporary theory of art objects insists on their radical individual character while accepting the possibility of some sort of intelligible (hermeneutic) discourse about this individuality. The belief that works of art are expressions of individual style obviously must rest on deeper beliefs about the individuality of human beings who create these objects. If human beings cannot be properly understood as individuals, then it would be anomalous if their products could be so understood. Art objects express an individuality; they are not the reality of that individuality. We must seek directly, then, for the basis of individual self-consciousness in Hegel.

If we remember that the root of individual self-consciousness is in the desire to possess a nonnatural object, then Hegel's development of this notion in the *Phenomenology* proceeds quite "logically."

Immediately after the section which locates the first sentiments of self in man as a desiring creature, Hegel turns to the famous analysis of master and slave. If our search is for individual self-consciousness, then it is in the primitive desire of the master to possess the *nonnatural* object which is another human consciousness that we will find the roots of individuality—and the fundamental dialectic of history. In what sense is the situation of master and slave properly described as the master's possession of a *nonnatural* object? Isn't it simply begging the question to declare that the slave as a specimen of homo sapiens qualifies for this curious title?

The general influence of Kant's moral philosophy on Hegel's philosophical world would certainly have suggested at least the formula that the slave was a "nonnatural object." For Kant, freedom, which belongs essentially to all human beings, is nonnatural in the precise sense that it cannot be comprehended in the universal world of causality—nature—which he discusses in the *Critique of Pure Reason*. There are many reasons why Kant's developed theories are unsatisfactory for Hegel, but they would at least give an initial plausibility to the notion that slavery is "the possession" of a free (nonnatural) being. Since the basis of freedom in Kant is man's rationality, the Kantian machinery also helps to introduce reason into the root notion of history. In Hegel's view, history arises from the attempt to possess the freedom (reason) of another. Individuality arises from this desiring possession by a master of a nonnatural, free, rational object, a slave.

Kant's actual discussion of rationality in man is very different from Hegel's, and the attempt to justify Hegel via Kant is not only inaccurate in this case but is an attempt to justify one puzzling theory by another not less puzzling. The best way to comprehend what Hegel is after is to sketch briefly the fundamental situation of master and slave as he sees it. In what way can it be said to conform to the situation which he claims must occur if individual self-consciousness is to arise? First of all it is clear that the attitude of the master is that of a *desiring* consciousness. He does not view the other as a mere object to be known, but he sees him in a very practical context. We think of the slave as one who works for the master and thus carries out practical desires which the master sets for him. If this is the limit of our concept of slavery, however, we would fail to understand Hegel's account of master and slave and how it relates to historical consciousness. If the master dominates the slave just for practical service, then the slave would be a mere tool to be understood on the logic of tools. The slave would be like a domestic animal and would be understood wholly under the categories of nature. As we noted above in discussing naturalistic theories of culture, these fail to support the interest in individual self-consciousness that Hegel believes to be at the root of history. If the slave exists only as a means to serve natural ends, then we have no interest in him as an *individual*, any more than we have in the individual character of any tool. The character of such tools is wholly in their universal form and function. What the master wishes from the slave is not service but recognition; he wishes to possess not the crafts or strengths of the other but his freedom. The fight which leads to the domination of the master is a fight for prestige. The desiring consciousness, then, does not want the fulfillment of any natural end—natural ends which simply lead consciousness back into the repetitive cycle of nature; desiring consciousness now wants a quite nonnatural end—recognition by the other, honor or prestige. If anyone has any doubts about the fact that we are in a different nonnatural world altogether when the struggle is for honor, only consider the pejorative interpretations offered of such battles. One of the repeated critiques of war and human conflict is based on the assertion of man as a *natural* being: why do men fight for flags and slogans, for personal and national honor, when what we need is food and love? Nature has no need for vanity; as *natural* beings we are alike in our common needs, not shut off in our selfish search for glory. The sooner man roots himself in nature and forgets the unnatural notions of honor, the better off the human race will be. This is a persuasive critique, but Hegel will have none of it, for the vision it finally yields of man is that of a benign and peaceful animal herd. The road to human self-consciousness is through conflict over nonnatural ends.

The search in this chapter has been for "subjective Reason," for that form of mental awareness which is appropriate for historical investigation, for the recognition of *historical* reality. We have insisted that the proper object of historical interest must be something individual, not generic, and that we must locate a "cognitive" interest in individuality if there is to be consciousness of historical events. Understanding was rejected because of its interest in universals, sense perception because it can only reach the abstract particular. We found it necessary to move to self-consciousness (through desiring consciousness) and to find the root of interest in individuality, the *recognition* of individuality in the conflict between master and slave. Where is reason in this process? We have already suggested where it lies in our Kantian formulations. Reason is the basis of human freedom. What the master desires is the freedom of the slave—not the freedom for some purpose—he wants that freedom itself in the act of recognition. The object of the master's desiring consciousness is the reason-freedom-self-consciousness of the other, and he wishes to "possess" that reason in the other in order to affirm his own freedom-reason-self-consciousness. His desiring consciousness becomes nonnatural and truly individual because he seeks as his object something which he regards as nonnatural, free, and individual: the consciousness of the other rational being. Only rational beings can be the objects of historical interest because only rational beings are free, are individuals (objective reason); only rational beings can have historical consciousness and recognize the individuality which is the basis of history (subjective reason). "To him who looks at the world rationally, the world looks rationally back."

As suggested previously, Hegel's use of reason may seem somewhat idiosyncratic since we normally think of reason as the mental faculty associated with abstract science—the world of the understanding. There is considerable historical warrant for Hegel's use of reason, not only in Kant's analysis of practical reason and the role of reason in establishing the freedom and dignity of the human person, but in the dialectics of pure reason where Kant denies reason the capability which Hegel asserts for it: the ability to grasp reality as a summed, individual object. For Kant, reason would be the proper faculty to grasp the great undivideds, the ultimate individuals which are not understood as mere instances of generic categories since they merge universal and instance, essence and existence. The prime candidates for *individual* in Kant are the soul, the world, and God. For Kant they cannot be understood under the normal logic of universal concept (the world of the understanding) so they cannot be known at all. Hegel is not so shy. To discuss why and how individuality as such can be known in any extent is a massive procedure, and this commentary will rely finally on some intuitive notions to justify Hegel's position. But in assessing his claims about reason in history we must be clear that reason is the peculiar faculty which creates and recognizes individual self-consciousness and, therefore, *historical* reality as Hegel conceives it. "[S]elf-consciousness is Reason.... [When Reason discovers that] the individuality of consciousness is seen to be in itself absolute reality, it discovers the world as its own new and real world."[23]

This concludes our general discussion of objective and subjective reason in history, and it should be clear from the discussion why the subjective/objective distinction finally collapses in Hegel's treatment. Before turning to the use which Hegel makes of these general notions about reason, it might be well to offer a brief comment on the common-sense outcome of these dialectics. I believe that the repeated emphasis on individuality as a particular historical interest conforms to our common-sense views about history, no matter how we may evaluate it. Hegel's development of historical consciousness in the battle between master and slave strongly suggests that he sees the dominant and proper subject of history to be political history. The proper interest of history arises in how men manage their freedom in social groups. Political history cannot, for instance, be reduced to economic history in Hegel (thus he is no Marxist) because economic history is infected with naturalistic determinants. What interests us *historically* is not how men have met their basic needs through tools and trade, but how men have regarded one another's freedom and dignity—a political problem. The traditional focus of practicing historians on political history is not accidental, then, since it is only in the political context, where men pit their freedom against one another, that historical interest can be generated.

To understand the edifice of universal history and the process of
its construction, one must know the materials that were used to
construct it. Those materials are men. To know what *history* is,
one must know who man who realizes it is. Most certainly,
man is something quite different from a brick. In the first place,
if we want to compare universal history to the construction of
an edifice, we must point out that men are not only the bricks...
used in the construction; they are also the masons who build it
and the architects who conceive the plan for it; a plan, moreover,
which is progressively elaborated during the construction itself.
Furthermore, even as "brick," man is essentially different from a
material brick: even the human brick changes during construction, just as the human mason and the human architect do.
Nevertheless, there is something in man, in every man, that makes
him suited to participate—passively or actively—in the realization
of universal history.
　　Finally, man is not only the material, the builder, and the
architect of the historical edifice. He is also the one *for whom*
this edifice is constructed: he lives in it, he *sees* and *understands*
it, he *describes* and *criticizes* it.[1]

This passage is Kojève's general comment on chapter 6 of the
Phenomenology. If one compares his metaphor of the "edifice of
universal history" with the extended quotation on reason with which
Hegel commenced his 1830 lectures on world philosophical history,
one notes striking similarities. Kojève talks about "man" where
Hegel talks abstractly about reason, but the doctrine is the same:
History is man/reason's peculiar "edifice." What particularly
interests me, however, is the resort in both accounts to the Aristotelian four causes. I have already pointed out the italicization of the
causal concepts in Hegel's manuscript. In Kojève's statement, the
same dimensions are again stated: man is material cause (brick);

efficient cause (mason); formal cause (architect); final cause (the one for whom the edifice of history exists). Neither Hegel nor Kojève credits Aristotle for offering the basic schematism of their statements on reason or man in history, and there is no specific reason why they should. Although there are many nice philosophical problems about the four causes, they do seem to have a certain common-sense currency and value. In discussing houses—whether actual mansions or the edifice of history—we do fall into taking up just the factors which Hegel points to in his initial claims about reason and which Kojève picks up in his explanatory metaphor. Because of the common-sense character of the four causes, I will not offer any analysis of Aristotle's actual doctrine beyond a few minor comments as I proceed in elucidating Hegel. I want to emphasize, however, the fact that something like the four causes exists as the basic framework for Hegel's initial thesis, because it seems clear that these causal dimensions are the principles used for the articulation of the text of *Reason in History*.

In the last three chapters I have tried to characterize what *kind* of study Hegel thought he was undertaking in *Reason in History* and then attempted to outline some of the dimensions of the basic notion of reason. I will now turn to how he uses these general notions to offer an account of historical reality. I do not intend in this commentary to enter into his actual application of his categories to the historical record—this application constitutes the bulk of the *Lectures on the Philosophy of History*. What we will be examining next are the factors which Hegel believes must enter into any properly historical account and which offer the proper conceptual schematism for understanding historical reality. History, we discover, must be understood as it displays reason in the four causal dimensions: reason as end (freedom, the individuality of peoples); reason as means (passion, the world historical individual); reason as subject matter (states); reason as form (the constitutions: democratic, republican, monarchic).

The Structure of the Text of Reason in History

Hegel's initial statement about reason develops in three stages. First we are told that reason is the substance of history, then this is expanded in terms of the causes, and finally we are told that reason works itself out from potentiality to actuality. This order follows a general Aristotelian progression. The prime question in any inquiry is the substantial question: what is x? Hegel's question is: what is history? And we get the substantial answer: History is Reason. (Or, more conventionally: historical events are peculiarly rational events.) This substantial answer is then expanded by the analytic framework of the four causes which define substance. Finally, in the case of some substances (those involving change as a basic characteristic), Aristotle says that the causes operate in a schematism of potency and act: the formal cause is only potentially present in the seedling, and it is the actualization of the form which is the *telos* of the process. The quotation, then, roughly follows the discussion of an Aristotelian changeable substance. That in itself might be interesting, but what is most illuminating is that the actual textual order of *Reason in History* carries out the three stages stated in the initial quotation.

The text of the 1830 lectures is broken up into subsections as follows (the subheads a, b, c, etc. are manuscript material):

A. Its [World History's] Universal Concept
B. The realization of spirit in history
    a) the determination of spirit
    b) the means of realization
    c) the material of realization
    d) its reality
C. The course of world history
    a) the principle of development
    b) the beginning of history
    c) the course of development[2]

Roughly speaking, A deals with reason as substance, B with reason and the four causes, and C with the dynamics of history—the working out of reason from potency to actuality. My attempt in the last two chapters on objective/subjective reason has been an attempt to give an explanation of and expansion on section A. In trying to define reason, we have been attempting to discuss in what sense reason is the "substance" of history. I now turn to sections B and C and discuss the causes, potency, and actuality.

In claiming that the schema of the causes is behind the organization of section B, any commentator could wish that Hegel had been more explicit on this matter. Nevertheless, even with the rambling character of the text, the causal schema still seems clearly discernible. I would align the causes with the subsections as follows:

a) determination of spirit   (final cause)
b) means of realization   (efficient cause)
c) material of realization   (material cause)
d) its reality   (formal cause)

Section B (a) in the Hoffmeister text is very different from the material which occurs at roughly this point in the Karl Hegel text. The general title is the same, but the Karl Hegel text is very brief and consists in a short discussion of the nature of spirit and discussion of freedom as the true *end* of history. In Hoffmeister, the discussion of spirit, and the fact that its essence is freedom, heads up the section but there follows a very extended discussion on the spirit of peoples which is rounded off, finally, by some closing remarks again on the problem of the spirit. It might seem that the discussion of *Volk* was not proper in discussing the *end* of history, but Hegel believes that the formation of the self-conscious community, a people, is the aim of historical action. These peoples, as we have already noted, are the proper individuals of history. Thus, one can properly say that it is the formation of individuality in the form of peoples which is the aim of history or "the determination of the Spirit." The discussion of peoples, then, as the ideal form of social organization toward which history works is altogether appropriate.

B (b) is concerned with the "means" (*Mittel*) of realization and begins with the general assertion that spirit uses the passions of individuals as the means of advance. These, Hegel says, are the only real drives that operate in history, and he contrasts the effectiveness of passion with the ineffectiveness of mere ideals and rational belief. Passion as the effective force in history is not raw passion, however, which he says falls outside the scope of history. It is passion which has been qualified, molded, formed, guided by the idea. The union of passion and the idea, which he calls the warp and woof of history, constitutes the moral reality—the state—for men. It may be difficult then, to be sure whether the efficient cause (means) for the realization of reason is passion, the idea, or the state. Nevertheless, it is the general message of the section that passion alone actually *moves* history, and therefore it seems fair to think that in this section he is dealing with efficient causality in contrast to the end of freedom which was discussed in the previous section. The fact that B (b) contains his discussion of the history-maker par excellence, the world historical individual, is a further confirmation of his interest here in the efficient cause.

B (c) is obviously the easiest to identify with one of the causes since the title directly alludes to material causality: "In human knowledge and will the rational comes to existence as in a material element."[3] Having noted this basic material substrate, he then turns immediately to the more proximate matter of history, which is the state, and an extended discussion of the state ensues. Finally, B (d) should be by elimination about "formal" cause, and in general this is borne out by the section which is concerned with constitutions, variously referred to by him as *Staatsform* or *Gestalt*.[4]

Not only are the causes used to mark the basic breaks in the text, but it also seems that there is a kind of rough progression from a through d. Having given us the general concept of reason in section A, Hegel turns in section B to how reason is expressed in the actual dimensions of history. Reason exists at this state of the argument merely as an idea which is first of all posited as the end toward which history is moving. He then asks how that end is to be realized and he discusses the efficient causality in history. The union of the efficient cause (human passion) with the end to be achieved (the idea) yields the basic matter or content of history (the state), which in turn expresses itself in the form of a proper constitution. Even in rough form the suggested structure should be a help in following Hegel's theory. *Reason in History* is frequently regarded as a disconnected set of striking claims rather than a work with a reasonably clear-cut developmental pattern. It seems to me that Hegel virtually outlines his own book in the famous initial quotation on reason and then, proceeds, in fact, to fill in the outline. It is always some advance to show that a philosopher had a plan in mind when he wrote his work and was not just assembling idle inspirations.

Before proceeding directly to the various causes in history some remarks must be made about confusions that can arise in applying the causal scheme. One confusion that strikes most readers is the overlapping of the causal specifications. Here, for instance, is a shift within one paragraph:

> [Freedom] is the ultimate purpose toward which all world history has continually aimed.... Freedom alone is the purpose which realizes and fulfills itself, the only enduring pole in the change of events and conditions, the only true efficient principle.[5]

Is freedom then the final cause or the efficient cause? If it is the efficient cause, how does it relate to the later claim that passions are the sole drives (*Triebfedern*) in history (and, the Karl Hegel text adds, "the main efficient cause")?[6] But if passion is the efficient cause, we are then told that the *material* cause of history is the subjective wills of men, their passions and private interests. All of these overlappings are, of course, only reflections of the initial quotation which locates reason at all dimensions of the causal analysis. At this stage all I wish to do is note this overlapping; in the actual commentary on the causes I will try to show how it is that freedom, the passions, the state, and so on are all fundamentally "rational" in Hegel's sense so that this shifting of terms from one pole to the other of the causal framework is legitimate and necessary.

A second confusion that occurs is like the first but slightly different. We have just seen above how a term like "freedom" can appear in a single paragraph as final purpose and efficient principle. The other thing which Hegel does that is confusing is to change the specification of a cause. Thus, the final purpose of history may be variously stated as reason, spirit, the idea, freedom, self-consciousness, and so on. The apparent confusion of terms arises from the fact that Hegel sees these various notions (in the case of final cause) as "analytically" related. The end of history is spiritual activity that is rational activity, that is, the activity of freedom, which is defined as a kind of individual self-consciousness. Hegel slips back and forth between these denominations of final cause with seeming indifference and I have often followed suit. Again, part of the actual analysis of section B will involve tracing some of these analytic relations. To someone who fails to realize the close interrelation between the key Hegelian terms, however, the change of nomenclature can easily cause confusion.

The organization of the text which I have outlined according to the causes seems to me clearly presented in Hoffmeister's edition, and, insofar as this is the best edition we are likely to get out of the sources, I take it as definitive. The Karl Hegel text from which Hartman's translation was made displays the causal schematism but in a more jumbled fashion. As I have noted, the Hoffmeister German text and the available English translation often diverge widely in the arrangement of materials, and much more is included in Hoffmeister than is found in Hartman. If my aim in this work was a detailed *explication de texte*, then the anomaly of commenting for

English readers on the English translation of an imperfect German text via another, better, untranslated edition of the "same" material would be striking. There would be nothing to do but offer a translation of Hoffmeister's edition and then proceed to comment. I hope that someone will offer us an English version of the Hoffmeister text, but I believe that there is value in the present line of investigation. The basic *doctrine* of the Karl Hegel edition and of the Hoffmeister version is, as far as I can judge, the same. Hegel is nothing if not a repetitious writer. He is constantly reiterating his basic notions in different forms and guises. Thus, whether we have a discussion of freedom as the end of history, or a discussion of peoples as the end of history, there is no change in basic doctrine; it is a different way of describing the same theory. Given the textual situation, I have not attempted in the discussions of sections B and C to comment on every line and twist of argument in either text. I have attempted, instead, to state what seems to me the central doctrine (which is the same in both editions), to show its importance and how it should be understood. All of the texts are very patchy, so that in a single paragraph one moves from flowing rhetoric to intricate doctrine derived from Hegel's logical writings. There are interesting and bewildering digressions that I have avoided both from a desire to construct a clear line of argument and often from my own inability to discover exactly what they mean. With these textual caveats I will proceed to the discussion of final cause in history.

Final Cause: Freedom and History

> The history of the world is the progress in the consciousness of freedom . . . the final cause of the world [is] the consciousness by Spirit of its freedom and the . . . realization of its freedom.[7]

I begin with final cause since that is where Hegel begins, but a few preliminary remarks about the general relation of final and efficient causality are in order. The plausibility of *any* analysis by means of final cause is greatly enhanced by one's views on the efficient causality of the process in question. In the case of artificial objects specification of final cause is not only quite acceptable but is almost the first question one asks. "What is it for?" we want to know when shown some new tool or artifact. (Even objects of the fine arts submit easily to final causality; thus all the commotion about the *meaning* of the arts.) On the other hand, search for final cause seems immediately far less plausible when dealing with objects which are not man-made, for example, natural objects. "What is the final cause of the cork tree?" "Bottle stoppers," says a parody of Aristotle. In terms of the causes, we say that, given certain efficient causes (men), we admit the dimension of final causality; but, given other efficient causes (nature), we are inclined to question final causality. If it is the case that artificial objects admit easily of "final" causality—indeed they seem to require it—then it is important to emphasize that for Hegel history is an *artificial* creation.

This is a point which has already been made from many perspectives: the insistence on the nonnatural (nonrepetitive, progressive) character of historical reality; historical reality as the creation of reason; historical reality, in Kojève's terms, as man's peculiar "edifice." If history is man-made, then it would seem to require a final cause. If history is not clearly differentiated from natural process, then the search for final causality becomes just that much less plausible because of our doubts about final cause in nature. Finally, in the definitions often given for "speculative philosophies of history," a search for a pattern in all the events that ever happened, one can see the final evaporation of the distinctions which make Hegel's quest plausible. As speculative philosophies of history are frequently understood, they involve a search for the final cause of all historical events, where "historical" has lost all *descriptive* content. In such speculative philosophies of history, "historical" has a metaphysical or logical use in that it contrasts to possible or imaginary events. History is what actually happened: the world as the totality of what is the case, the facts. But if historical means what actually happened as against what might have happened, then to say that an event is historical is not to add any descriptive information; it is to say that the event is actual or that it exists. And, as Kant says, "existence" is not a descriptive predicate. Hegel's search for the meaning of history is a search for the final cause of certain kinds of man-made events as contrasted to natural events or chance occurrences. "Historical" added to "event" is, then, a descriptive predicate which designates a limited subset of the totality of events.

If one keeps in mind the close relationship between final and efficient causality along with the fact that, for Hegel, "historical" is a descriptive term designating a limited subset of events, then one can reassess the relation between his philosophy of history and providential searches for the "meaning of history." When Hegel says that history has a final cause, we ask at once who "made" history (efficient cause), and many immediately assume that the only appropriate answer is "God." There is all that talk about the spirit, and the text ends with a heavy theological swell which asserts that his philosophy is a true theodicy.[8] The identification of God as the artificer of history will be greatly assisted by failure to note Hegel's own critical distinction between events in general and historical events. Historical events are, as we have just reiterated, only a subset (and statistically a rather minor subset) of events in general. If one asks what is the efficient cause of *all* events, everything that has ever happened or will happen, then certainly a Divine Being seems the only appropriate culprit. But, if historical events constitute only a sharply limited class of events, it might be regarded as impious to give God jurisdiction over such a meager portion. This point is very important: the introduction of a theological perspective (particularly a Christian theological perspective) into Hegel's philosophy of history will immediately endanger the critical analytic distinction of his whole analysis, the distinction between nature and spirit. The Christian God is traditionally Lord of nature (Creator) and of history (Savior), and the temptation of any consistent-minded theologian will be to try to reduce the principles which Hegel has held apart to a single unity lest God turn out to be a logical contradiction. Either nature is given a history, in which case we cannot draw easily Hegel's distinction between nature and history; or man is regarded as having some definite "nature" (perhaps a *super*-nature), in which case history becomes an empty illusion since man's task is essentially "natural," that is, to achieve his nature.[9]

A more appropriate interpretation of Hegel would be to specify the artificer of history as man, not God. Historical events as a special subclass of events are events marked by a certain kind of human making. If events are shaped in a certain way by human design, we can indeed ask what the purpose of this making has been, so that the admission of final causality in historical events does not violate common sense. If one loses sight of the restricted nature of the class of *historical* events, then the notion of man as the maker of history is bizarre. Nor is it even all human actions that are in question but only those human actions which are "shaped" in a certain fashion, that is, those which relate to the formation of peoples or states.

> The realm of the Spirit consists in what is produced [*hervorge-bracht*] by man. One may have all sorts of ideas about the Kingdom of God; but it is always a realm of Spirit to be realized and brought about in man.[10]

Having emphasized the Aristotelian separation of art and nature as a means of making Hegel's search for a final cause in history more plausible, it is important to turn right about and point to the peculiarities of Hegelian history as an "artificial" object when contrasted to a product of Aristotelian *techne*. For Aristotle "art imitates nature," and from the standpoint of our analysis of history the imitation is rather too slavish. Aristotle seems to pass back and forth with ease between analysis of natural and artificial objects; in the *Physics*, a treatise on natural change, he continuously uses artificial objects—statues, bronze spheres, and so on—to illustrate his points. Doctoring is an artificial process to be sure, but this means that the doctor substitutes himself for the natural *efficient* cause and that his therapy very directly imitates natural process. The simple example of artificial process is when a man has some form or final cause in mind and acts as the efficient cause to bring that form to being in a material—one thinks of the carpenter making the bed, the doctor producing health, the horticulturist pruning his plants. While all these processes are indeed "artificial," they are *too* imitative of natural process to serve as models for history in Hegel. In my judgment many of the misreadings of Hegel come about from applying improper models of "artificial" change to Hegel's account of history. These misinterpretations subtly introduce schematisms appropriate to *nature*, or to art imitating nature, into Hegel and they will not serve for history.

One way of drawing out the peculiar character of Hegel's search for a final cause in history is to contrast his investigation with a similar-sounding theory but one based finally on a specification of final cause which is borrowed from natural teleology. As we already know, Hegel specifies the final cause in history as the realization of freedom and reason. He was not the first philosopher to make such a claim. The notion was, in fact, a rather popular one in the period of the Enlightenment. Condorcet's *Sketch for the Progress of the Human Mind*[11] is a particularly fine example of the view that history is inevitably progressing toward enlightenment, the overthrow of tyrants, and the establishment of a regime of reason and freedom. Part of the difficulty in reading Hegel is that it is so easily assumed that Hegel's dense prose really comes out to the same conclusion as that of the lucid Frenchman. Nothing could be farther from the truth. Using the analysis which we have already made of the special meaning of reason in Hegel's philosophy of history, let us look at the difference between Hegel's and the Enlightenment's search for an end for history.

Any teleology which Condorcet introduces into history is a teleology which is in fact a *natural* teleology. In this case it is the nature of man, his nature as a rational being which determines the necessary outcome of history. If human reason is understood under the model of natural teleology, then man as a rational being will have to be understood as natural beings are understood in Hegel: as an instance of a universal type. So it is for Condorcet. Rational man is man as a universal—this is the basis of the cosmopolitanism of Enlightenment political theory. All men everywhere are the same insofar as they share in the universal character of reason. History will eventually yield to human nature, and the kingdom of reason and freedom will be established: that is the message of Condorcet's doctrine of progress. Here we have *natural* necessity working itself out in time, in history. The trouble with such a theory, from Hegel's point of view, is that it has no real philosophy of *history*. There is no reason in history, reason is in the nature of man while actual history, the ancien régime, for example, is profoundly irrational and contrary to human nature. For Condorcet, the philosopher-politician-revolutionary adopts a therapeutic position in history; he cures historical situations of their irrationalities and restores man to his rational nature.

The root of the Enlightenment view of human reason and history is Cartesian. Descartes looks for the real essence, the nature, of man by removing all the circumstances which determine him as René Descartes and discovering in the *cogito*, the *I* which thinks, the ineradicable root of human beings as rational creatures. The cogito is to the individual, René Descartes, and all other named individuals, as the universal concept in the understanding is to any instance of that concept, as in the idea of a triangle to any actual triangle. From Hegel's point of view this Cartesian notion is profoundly unhistorical (something on which Descartes would readily have agreed). The Cartesian method says in effect that all the traits which define me as a particular self, René Descartes, are doubtful, not wholly real, and that what is indubitably real is an I which thinks. This is an impersonal, transcendental self, not any historical personage. For Hegel, in sharp contrast, the particularly *human* lies in the value granted to the historical self which Descartes wants to escape in order to find some transhistorical human essence. Human nature and human freedom are posited *historically* for Hegel because it is the historical *individual* which is reason's special interest.

It is vitally important, therefore, to differentiate these two theories which state that "rational freedom" is the end toward which history points. When one works according to the Enlightenment formulations based on the logic of the reason as understanding, one gets a theory which discounts the importance of empirical history. If one says that history moves toward the realization of the idea of freedom on the model of ideas and their concretization in the world of the understanding, then the working out of the idea must be regarded as a merely mechanical process in which the means and materials used are of no essential value. The triangle in the mind and the triangle on the blackboard are the same for the purposes of geometry; the reality of any realization lies in the idea behind it. Descartes, who admired mathematical methods, was prepared to think of man on the same model. The particular man, Descartes, Plato, or Hegel, is *real* insofar as he participates in the essence of man as a thinking being, but the individual instances are of no more interest than a chalk triangle or a brass triangle or a sand triangle are to the geometer.

The idea of freedom in Hegel's philosophy is essentially historical, however, and can only be comprehended by the categories of reason, which are different from the mathematical categories of the understanding. In the realm of reason the concretization of the idea is not a matter of indifference. The relation between the idea of freedom and its realization in history is akin to the relation of an artistic idea in the mind of an artist and its realization in the medium. There are aesthetic theorists, Croce and Collingwood (strangely enough, heavily influenced by Hegel), who seem to regard the actual making of a painting, for instance, as mechanical, the externalization of an idea already present in the mind of the artist. If this were the case, then an artist's idea would be akin to the geometrical idea of a triangle which is mechanically realized on the blackboard. This theory seems to be a misdescription of what actually goes on in the process of realizing some expressive idea in a medium. To quote one critic of the theory:

> It is hard to believe that mental images could be so articulated in all respects to anticipate the physical pictures to be realized on wall or canvas. For this would involve not merely foreseeing, but also solving, all the problems that will arise, either necessarily or accidentally, in the working of the medium; and not merely is this implausible, but it is even arguable that the accreditation of certain material processes as the media of art is bound up with their inherent unpredictability; it is just because these materials present difficulties that can be dealt with only in the actual working of them that they are so suitable as expressive processes.[12]

Unless one appreciates the special *historical* meaning of freedom in Hegel's philosophy, one can easily fall into the supposition of many of his critics that empirical history is mere appearance when compared to the idea in the mind of the world spirit. If we knew the idea in the mind of the world spirit ahead of time, well, the whole of history would be a boring working out of the idea. Just as the geometer uses his chalk sketches as crutches for our weak conceptual powers, so the historical record could easily be bypassed if we could grasp the idea. My own interpretation of Hegel, on the contrary, would be that one should imagine the world spirit to be like the artist who, when he finishes the canvas, is willing to sign it because he sees it as his idea; but that does not mean that he could have predicted the final structure or "short circuited" the actual painting and given us the "real" artistic idea that he had in his head. We say to the geometer, halfway through his chalk demonstration, "All right, I get the idea, you don't have to draw it out." We don't say to the artist, as he sketches along, "Oh, I see what you're up to, don't bother to finish it."

It is the central contention of this commentary that the doctrine of reason in history points to a peculiar interest in individuality rather than universality, and, on that score, Enlightenment theories of historical progress are, in fact, theories of natural teleology and natural necessity, not theories of historical teleology and historical necessity. This notion of reason and history as individuality seems to me borne out by the central doctrines of Hegel's philosophy, but there is good cause to see why interpreters would assume that Hegel really is interested in some schematism very much like Condorcet's. I have contended that Condorcet's theory would substitute "the universal" for historical individuality, that it would understand history on a natural model. If that is indeed the case, then what is one to make of the many statements in *Reason in History* about the rights of the idea and "the universal"? For example:

> [G]reat men seem only to follow their passion and their arbitrary wills. But what they pursue is the universal; that alone is their pathos. The particular in most cases is too trifling as compared with the universal; the individuals are sacrificed and abandoned. The Idea pays the tribute of existence and transience, not out of its own funds, but with the passions of individuals.[13]

Or consider this manuscript statement on "human nature" which occurs at the beginning of section B just before the final causality in history is discussed:

> [I]t is of interest, in the course of history, to learn to know spiritual nature in its existence . . . namely, human nature. In speaking of human nature we mean something permanent. The concept of human nature must fit all men and all ages, past and present. This universal concept may suffer infinite modifications; but actually the universal is one and the same essence in its most various modifications. Thinking reflection disregards the variations and adheres to the universal which under all circumstances is active in the same manner and shows itself in the same interest. The universal type appears even in what appears to deviate from it most strongly.[14]

Doesn't all this talk about "the universal" finally end up in discounting individual historical reality—the vice, we claim, of Enlightenment philosophies of history? Isn't it clearly Hegel's message that individuals are as nothing compared to the great "universal" purposes of world history?

The clue to Hegel's view is not difficult to discover. In the two passages first quoted, in which he is discussing the sacrifice of the individual in the interests of the "universal," the "universal" to which he refers is in fact the state or the people, the proper historical *individuals*. The sacrifices of individual men, both heroes and ordinary persons, are sacrifices in terms of the universal as it is embodied in the proper historical individual, the people. The particular individual is not lost in an abstraction, a nonhistorical

Cartesian essence, he is lost in the larger individual: the people. Individuality is sacrificed for individuality: particular individuality for universal individuality. To be sure, that may seem only a piece of verbal sleight of hand to many thinkers. To a modern Hegelian critic like Karl Popper, sacrifice of personal individuality to the larger "individual" of the state is nothing more than sacrifice of individuality to the "empty universal." Popper sees only individual human beings as real, and he regards the state as a logical fiction, an abstract essence for which the sacrifice of individual existence is completely unjustified. I will not at this point expound the justification for Hegel's curious view of the state as "a cultural individual," but it is worth pointing out that, in his own terminology, the universal which appears so often in *Reason in History* as the guiding principle of history is the *concrete* universal, the people, that is *the* individual.

The quotation on the unity and permanence of human nature which sounds so much like the abstract doctrines of rational essence that one expects to find in Enlightenment theories is *immediately* followed up in the text by a crucial Hegelian turn. In the Karl Hegel text: "This kind of reflection abstracts from the content, the purpose of human activity."[15] In Hoffmeister the text reads:

> If we see, for example, a man kneeling down and praying to an idol, and if we regard the content as something which reason rejects, still we can grasp the feeling which is a living one and can say that the feeling has the same worth as that of a Christian who worships in the splendor of truth and as the philosopher absorbed with thinking Reason in the eternal truth.... If we take this attitude in general, then we can say that there is no necessity to go into the great theatre of world history. It is a well known anecdote regarding Caesar, that he could have met the same aspirations and deeds in a small town as he saw in the great show place of Rome. The same inclinations and exertions are found in a small city as in the great world theatre. We see that in these kinds of observations one abstracts from the content, the aim of human activity. This exceptional indifference contrary to a sense of real objectivity one finds particularly in the French and English; these are the very same ones who are called philosophical writers of history.[16]

Hegel is certainly correct that the kind of reflections he is suggesting are often regarded as philosophical attitudes toward history par excellence. Many people do have the notion that a philosophical approach to history is necessarily made from the standpoint of some overall view about the general nature of human beings: as rational, as desiring, as economic, and so on. In terms of the general nature of man, it is then possible to understand all the various concrete actions as expressions of this basic nature. If one says that the nature of man is to be ambitious, then Alexander's ambition to conquer Asia and the stock boy's ambition to rise in the firm become the *same* phenomenon. One abstracts from the aim or content of the ambition in terms of a general theory of human behavior. Such theories are enormously attractive because they are true *theories* of history in which the whole vast, complex content of the past is ironed out in terms of a powerful explanatory model. As theories of history they seem to give us what philosophy should supply, a universal pattern in the past. To put Hegel's views in the boldest fashion, it seems to me that he would reject the notion that there could be any *theory* of history in a sense comparable to theory as it is used in the natural sciences. One has theories when there are universal objects subject to explanatory laws: none of those conditions are met in historical reality.

To return directly to the question, then, of the final cause in history, we must understand that, if it is stated as the fulfillment of reason, the final cause must be understood not as the attainment of some universal essence of man which could have been known by some intellectual intuition (as in Descartes) prior to or outside of actual historical process. All such views of human nature or human reason are merely formalistic. The final state of Enlightenment history must be a cosmopolitanism: the universal state based on the single rational essence of man. Hegel's view might better be called a "polypolitanism." Given the view of a common, intuitable human nature, Enlightenment politics can give no satisfactory account for the plurality of states.[17] How can it be that, given this universality of human nature, man has divided himself into all these separated polities? The basic answer is "irrationalism"—loyalty to dynasties, outmoded religions, foolish customs. In the final end of history, when man realizes his universality, there will be a universal state. Hegel also seems to be interested in a world government, but he does not view the many states and peoples of history as irrationalities. They are the primary products of reason, since reason constructs concrete individual cultures, not the vacuous, universal utopias of the Enlightenment. Thus, having rejected the "contentless" universality of the French and English "philosophers of history," Hegel's first assertion when he turns to discuss "The determination of the Spirit," that is, final cause, is:

> We say now about [the determination of the spirit] that it is not an abstract thing, not an abstraction such as human nature, but it is something thoroughly individual, active, altogether living.[18]

The end of history in Enlightenment thought must be measured to the nature of man. Man's nature is ahistorical, it is discovered by rational intuition and amounts to some variation on the impersonal cogito which Descartes discovers in his inner meditations. The end of history, then, is the transcendence of the individualities, both personal and social, of human existence. Human reality is not located in *self*-consciousness and individual existence, it is located only in rational essence. To live in the Enlightenment utopia would be like attending a congress of scientists in which all that is particular drops away and the sole activity is the interchange of cognitive awareness. The end of history for Hegel, however, is individual through and through. The aim of history is to maximize *self*-consciousness; the development of individuality is the only aim that history could have. If there is a meaning in historical instances as instances, in the particularity of historical fact, then it is because all these individualities are of value. Enlightenment philosophies of history really end in denying that history has meaning, purpose, or final end because, given the logic of the understanding, they can locate no value in individual reality.

When human beings make history (either in the sense of doing deeds or thinking historically) they do so in order to produce self-consciousness. The aim of historical making is something individual and self-conscious. Thus, it is more than appropriate that, in Hoffmeister's arrangement of the text, the section on the "determination" of the spirit, or the aim of history, should be given over to Hegel's extended discussion of peoples. Since peoples are the true historical individuals, it must be peoples which are the aim of historical making. Peoples are the aim of historical deeds in the sense that it is in terms of the forming of such communities that historical deeds are done; peoples are the aim of historical narrations since it is only in the desire for social self-consciousness that historical narration arises.

It seems to me that Hegel has a very powerful case in arguing that if historical reality, individuality, has any purpose then this purpose must be something individual, historical. The end of historical reality should be completely commensurate with the manner and means of its making, and everyone would seem to admit that history is the doings of particular individuals. The historical work of these individuals can hardly be properly realized in some universal or transcendent goal. If self-consciousness has a purpose, it hardly seems that this purpose can be some Cartesian existence which obliterates self-consciousness. Translating the thesis into the world of historical narration: if historical writing has any *intrinsic* purpose, then it must be because we think there is some irreplaceable value in the particularity of the record. We cannot believe that the many histories are so many case studies for the ultimate sociology. What is peculiar about Hegel's theory is not so much the interest in individuality, it is the location of individuality in states or peoples. There might be a number of people who would say that somehow history is useful in knowing about ourselves, but they would likely be happier about that in a personalistic rather than a political context. Much of modern existentialism, for instance, is very keen on the radical historicity of human beings, but this is almost always given a personal interpretation. In fact, from the point of view of much of existentialism, states and peoples are abstract, impersonal, transcendent entities which block the free response of persons. I will not discuss the reasons for locating proper *historical* individuality in states and peoples here; I will attend to that when I discuss the proper subject matter of history in the next chapter. All I wish to do here is to show why individuality must be the aim of *historical* making.

A final remark about the end of history. I have not shown so far why there is anything like progress in history or why there should be any continuity of cultural development. One might well accept that men acted and thought *historically* in order to create self-consciousness in themselves or in their societies and that there would then be a kind of historical *telos* in any cultural development which attempted to maximize individual or collective self-awareness. There might be many "progresses" toward many self-realizations. Each of these processes would certainly be teleological, but that would hardly show what Hegel apparently wants to show, a continuity of cultures and a progress over many thousands of years from one people to another. That is a difficult thesis to substantiate indeed, and we will postpone it until we discuss the doctrine of progress in the next chapter.

Efficient Cause: Passion and the World Historical Individual

Having summed up the final end of history as freedom, Hegel asks how this idea is to be brought about. The answer he gives seems curious indeed.

> The question of the means whereby Freedom develops itself into a world leads us directly to the phenomenon of history. Although Freedom as such is primarily an internal idea, the means it uses are the external phenomena which in history present themselves directly to our eyes. The first glance at history convinces us that the actions of men spring from their needs, their passions, their interests, their characters and their talents.... It is true that this drama involves also universal purposes, benevolence or noble patriotism. But such virtues and aims are insignificant on the broad canvas of history.[19]

He goes on to say that it is true that the ideals of reason may be realized in certain individuals who adopt these benevolent notions but that "private aims, passions and the satisfaction of selfish desires"[20] far outweigh the effects of such noble beliefs. The true power of the passions lies

> in the fact that they respect none of the limitations which law and morality would impose upon them; that these natural impulses are closer to the core of human nature than the artificial and troublesome discipline that tends toward order, self-restraint, law and morality.[21]

Then, lest there be any doubt about the central role of passion as *the* effective force in history, Hegel nominates as the history-makers per se people whom he calls "world historical individuals." These great personages like Alexander, Caesar, and Napoleon act from no consciously noble motive:

> such men may treat other great and sacred interests inconsiderately—conduct which indeed subjects them to moral reprehension. But so mighty a figure must trample down many an innocent flower, crush to pieces many things in its path.[22]

What connection can this hymn to passion and immorality have to Hegel's general claim that reason is the alpha and omega of historical change?

One can understand the role of passion in history and how it relates to reason by considering carefully one of the most famous quotations from *Reason in History*:

> We assert that nothing has been accomplished without an interest on the part of those who brought it about. And if "interest" be called "passion"—because the whole individuality is concentrating all its desires and powers... on one subject—we may affirm that *nothing great in the world* has been accomplished without passion.[23]

The statement sounds more like the proclamation of a wild romantic or an embittered realist than a philosopher who started off asserting that reason is the sole actor in history. However, if one goes beyond the rhetoric of the passage, it is clear that passion has a necessary connection to Hegel's overall view of history and reason. Hegel defines the interest which moves history as a passion because "the whole individuality is concentrating its desires and powers." Our extended discussion of history and individuality should be recalled in this statement about "passion," therefore. Nor is this reference to individuality a mere phrase. He says:

> "Passion," it is true is not quite the right word for what I want to express. I mean here nothing more than human activity resulting from private interest, from special or, if you will, self-seeking designs—with this qualification: that the whole energy of will and character is devoted to the attainment of one aim and that other interests or possible aims, indeed everything else is sacrificed to this aim. This particular objective is so bound up with the person's will that it alone entirely determines its direction and is inseparable from it. It is that which makes the person what he is. For a person is a specific existence. He is not man in general—such a thing does not exist—but a particular human being.[24]

Passion, then, becomes a term which is linked to the expression of "the whole individuality" of a particular person. If passion and individuality are linked in this analytic fashion, then it seems that an interest in historical reality as individual reality must pay attention to "passion." In the previous chapter, I traced the origin of *self*-consciousness through the route of desire which "positions" the abstract, cognitive consciousness as a self. We noted that desire as such, however, need not produce proper self-consciousness. The passion or desire which is the efficient cause of history cannot have as its object merely natural ends: food, sex, natural life. Hegel reiterates this doctrine:

> The human agents have before them limited aims, special interests. But they are also intelligent, thinking beings. Their purposes are interwoven with general and essential considerations of law, the good, duty, etc. For mere desire, volition in its raw and savage form, falls outside the scene and sphere of world history.[25]

If the road to individual value, to self-consciousness, is through desire, then the means for the realization of history as self-consciousness must also be through specifically *human* desires. It would seem illogical to expect that self-consciousness could arise from acts which lacked self-interest, and so Hegel goes to some length to argue that the purposes of history can only be realized through the self-regarding actions of individual human beings. The universal moral motives of Enlightenment philosophers can have no historical import. It is not simply that such disinterested actions are statistically rare, it is rather that as disinterested they fail to assert individual self-consciousness and are therefore historically empty.

In the discussion on passion in history, Hegel is arguing against Kant. Kant's theory of morality makes a sharp distinction between actions according to duty, which are acts according to reason and freedom, and acts that are self-interested. Selfless acts are moral; self-interested acts may conform to duty but they are not done from duty and hence do not earn moral approbation. With or without Kant's assistance, this distinction has passed into much general understanding of moral action, so that Hegel's approbation of the self-interested act has for many readers a decidedly amoral if not immoral cast. It is quite clear from the text that the world historical individual is bound by no narrow notions of morality, and by and large this entire discussion of passion and heroism is the most distasteful part of Hegel's theory for modern readers all too well aware of recent outrages committed by various self-nominated men of destiny. Nevertheless, despite the obvious risks of establishing "higher purposes" for world historical individuals, it is a position which he cannot avoid espousing.

From Hegel's point of view, it seems that Kant is saying that the final value of man rests on his freedom as a rational being. Verbally, that statement is one with which he could agree, but as Kant interprets the statement it is quite unacceptable for Hegel's needs. Hegel views Kant as an Enlightenment moralist, offering a morality of the understanding, not a morality of reason. For Kant, I am most human when most rational. But, to be rational is to act in conformity to the moral law, to remove all aspects of *my* situation and to act as a universal moral legislator. From Hegel's point of view, this kind of theory of moral action replicates in the ethical world the errors of the understanding in the theoretical world. (Note the parallelism: explaining individual instances by subsuming under physical law; justifying instances of conduct by subsuming under moral law. The parallelism in Kant is deliberate.) In short, when I act most humanly, most morally for Kant I cannot act *historically* because I cannot assert *self*-consciousness; I can only assert the universal moral consciousness of man as a rational being. This moral consciousness transcends historical progress. There is no inherent progress in moral vision, no history of moral consciousness. History written from the Kantian standpoint—a standpoint which makes him a true Enlightenment figure—is moralistic history. From the vantage point of an eternally given transcendent and universal morality, one can grade the ages of man on the basis of conformity to moral law. If man *is* his moral reason, then reason is not *in* history for Kant. (Although Kant did write a brief essay on "philosophy of history," his notion is essentially the same as Condorcet's, which was discussed previously. Man's nature is rational; therefore, since nature does not create faculties without purpose, reason must by the principles of *natural* teleology eventually express itself in the form of a world government and perpetual peace.)[26]

From the standpoint of Kant's philosophy, or the common man's notions about disinterested conduct, Hegel has no other choice except to see the assertion of self-consciousness as something which "transcends" morality. For Kant, self-interested conduct is always *below* morality, but for Hegel some self-interested conduct is *above* morality in asserting the infinite right of determinate self-consciousness. This line of argument about "transcending morality" is so apt to sound like a call to insanity to the ordinary reader that it is worth pointing out what a pervasive problem it seemed to the post-Kantian philosophers. Nietzsche searches for a superman who goes "beyond good and evil"; Kierkegaard calls for a "teleological suspension of the ethical" in the interests of recovering religious consciousness; Schelling looks to aesthetic experience as a higher good than morality. In one way or another, it could be argued, these philosophers were trying to solve the problem of Kant's ethical views; how can the highest value for man fail to include his peculiarity as an individual self-consciousness. As Kierkegaard might put it: it is not man in general who is saved but S. K. who is saved—and all that makes S. K. *this* person is his actual historical situation, so that it is his historical being which must enter into a redemptive relation with God who is given in history, Jesus Christ.

Kant's espousal of reason as the inherent value for man turns out, on Hegel's reading, to be an espousal of the understanding. A true doctrine of reason connects it with self-consciousness. If reason is the root of self-consciousness, then the dichotomy which Kant constructs between reason and passion must be overcome. Passion is the origin of self, since it is desire which calls the abstract cognitive intellect into *self*-awareness. As we saw that doctrine develop, desire that was aimed at nonnatural ends, at another human consciousness, produced self-consciousness in the full sense. The passion which moves history is a passion to possess the freedom of others; it is passion for those aspects of reality which Hegel denominates spirit—self-consciousness—reason.

> Two elements therefore enter into our investigation: first the Idea, secondly, the complex of human passions; the one the warp, the other the woof of the vast tapestry of world history. Their contact and concrete union constitutes moral liberty in the state.[27]

Passion is the efficient cause of human action: mere ideas move nothing. Passion seeking the idea, reason, is history's motive force. Passion is also a kind of material cause which is formed by the idea, or reason. "In human knowledge and will, as in a material, Reason comes into existence."[28] Passion is what identifies man as a particular, not a universal, cognitive consciousness; and passion directed at and by the idea (freedom and reason in the self-consciousness of the other) yields the individuality and self-consciousness which constitute the world of historical reality and the interest of historical consciousness.

If we speak generically about the human psyche, then it is passion (desire) which is the efficient cause of all human actions; certain kinds of passions in certain situations generate historical action. When Aristotle discusses efficient causality, his question is most naively put in the form of who (or what) made this thing. The father is the efficient cause of the child (women are mere passive matter); the artist is the cause of the artifact. It may have been the parent's passion or the artist's desire for fame which moved each of them to action, but they are the specified efficient causes. In this section on the means used by spirit to develop itself in history, Hegel makes just such a specific identification of the efficient cause, the artificer in history: the world historical individual. If one asks who makes history in the same sense as one would ask who makes chairs, the answer is certain particular people, the history shapers, the heroes of the human story. Hero worship is not much favored in the twentieth century, and many readers are likely to be made distinctly uncomfortable by Hegel's adulation of Alexander, Caesar, and Napoleon. It is probably not possible to dispel all this discomfort, but it is possible to indicate why the world historical individual is necessary to Hegel's view of historical reality.

At the risk of repeating my central thesis beyond the point of diminishing returns, I must point out again that it is absolutely necessary for Hegel that the efficient cause of history share the particular character of historical reality: the world historical individual is an *individual*. If the aim of history is the realization of some sort of self-consciousness, then the maker of history himself must have some level of self-consciousness; if the aim is an individualized reality, then it must issue from something individual. I have repeatedly pointed to the analogy between historical reality and the individuality which we believe is the important aspect of works of fine art. We assume that these individualized objects which we read for their particular, nonuniversalizable characteristics must be the expressions of individualized self-consciousness. Theories of history which postulate the source of change in history as "vast impersonal forces" can hardly serve for Hegel's notion of historical reality. Freud may argue that there are certain pervasive passions which goad the artist on to his work. Da Vinci may well have been impelled to create certain forms by his various Oedipal problems, but, as Freud himself is the first to admit, nothing that the psychologist can say about these anonymous forces from the id can account for Da Vinci's genius. Presumably, many artists are pushed by dark, psychic forces, but in Da Vinci these forces are finally

shaped into an individual style, unmistakably his own and thorough-
ly under his control. In others we get undistinguished (and often
undistinguishable) forms and patterns which can equally well be
traced to the same psychic tensions that troubled Da Vinci. If I am
correct, then, that historical reality is uniquely individual in some
manner similar to the way a work of art is individual, we must
assume that in some fashion it issues from human beings who are
not merely the pawns of impersonal forces but stamp their
"product" with an individual vision.

To say that the efficient cause of history can be found in world
historical individuals like Alexander and Caesar requires careful
qualification. We must remember always that the proper individuals
in history are peoples. Finally, it is more proper to talk about states
as the efficient causes of history, but states must be regarded as
individuals, not as abstract ideas. States are individuals or "persons" writ large. If there were no particular men who could be said
to instantiate the self-consciousness of a state, then it would be
implausible to talk about the state as self-conscious or as an
individual. The state is no ghostly entity which has a ghostly mind
that the concrete individuals of the state cannot fathom. The world
historical individual is the one in whom or through whom the
individuality of the state is realized, at least partially. The ideal
situation would be one in which the personality of the state was
fully expressed in and through the person of a world historical
individual in full consciousness. Kojève gives this account of Hegel's
attitude toward Napoleon:

> Napoleon himself *is* the wholly "satisfied" Man, who, in and by
> his definite Satisfaction, completes the course of the historical
> evolution of humanity. He is the human *Individual* in the proper
> and full sense of the word; because it is through *him*, through *this*
> particular man, that the "common cause," the truly universal
> cause, is realized; and because this particular man is recognized,
> in his very particularity, by all men, universally.[29]

All that Napoleon lacks is "self-consciousness" of the fact of his
being "the human Individual," and that is what Hegel has attained.
Plato's ancient idea of the state summed up in the person of the
philosopher-king is split between Napoleon as king and Hegel as
philosopher.

We will discuss in the next chapter why proper individuality is
social for Hegel, but for now it is necessary to emphasize that the

Hegelian world historical individual is a *political* hero. Hegel's theory must not be confused with the various theories of genius or supermen which grew up in the nineteenth century. Many of those hero-worshipping theories were attempts to escape from history; the hero is likely to be the saint or artist who escaped the drabness of his age into a world of eternal values. Hegel's world historical figures are men who are responsible for the founding or revolutionizing of states. They can only be world *historical* individuals in that context because only states are the final history-bearers. Whatever prodigies of mysticism or morality an individual may accomplish in his inner life, these spiritual heroics are not of concern to world history. They may assert "subjective freedom," but they are "quite shut out from the noisy din of world history."[30]

We can illuminate the relation between the individuality of the world historical individual and the states he creates or destroys by taking a brief look at the basic dialectic of history in Hegel. As I noted in discussing the dialectic of methods of writing history, the standard pattern of dialectic progress in Hegel is for the last stage of the process to replicate at the level of mediacy what was accomplished immediately at the primary stage. World philosophical history replicates at the level of mediacy and self-consciousness what is merged immediately and naively at the level of original history. The world philosophical historian and the original historian are at one with the spirit of their subject matter. The original historian simply by writing about himself also writes about his state; the world philosophical historian by reflection on all of history also comes to understand himself as the self-consciousness produced by that history. A similar dialectic can be constructed for states and world historical individuals.

It is absolutely necessary for Hegel that the reality of history be individual and self-conscious (if these two notions are not in fact the same). He also thinks that history can be appropriately carried through only in societies. How can it be that societies can be thought of as individualized and self-conscious? The attribution of a Zeitgeist, a personality, to an age or culture has seemed to many Hegelian critics the merest anthropomorphism.[31] An obvious way of impressing a personality onto a society is to see the society as the extension of some individual. One could imagine the beginning of history, then, in the conquest of a society by a powerful individual who organizes all activities about his person. In the terms of the dialectic of master and slave, all in the society are slaves who offer him recognition. It is the self-consciousness, person, spirit of the ruler as master which organizes the society; all aspects of the society are determined by this act of self-recognition. Here there is no conflict between the person of the ruler and the spirit of the society; the Zeitgeist is *his* spirit, and one need not scruple to see the Periclean age as the personality and taste of Pericles writ large. (Not, I hasten to note, an appropriate example for Hegel, but the empirical truth is not at issue.) For Hegel, historical consciousness must "ideally" begin in such dominance. This is the immediate stage of history where the self of the world historical individual just *is* the self of the society.

Our previous discussion of the master/slave situation would indicate why the immediate stage of history breaks down. The personalized state based on the master's dominance over a community of slaves is based on an inner conflict which constantly threatens the central gesture of recognition upon which the state is based. The master (lord, king, hero) dominates the society and seeks to make the rule of his person the rule of the land, but his search for self-glorification (self-extension) can only be successful if in some sense the others in the society are regarded as free, individual selves. The master can only be *recognized* by other rational beings, not by animals. But how shall the conflict between the dominance of the master and the freedom of the slaves be resolved? That is the very story of history, for Hegel. The immediate unity of the state, which is merely the extension of the single master, breaks apart, and the historical record shows various modes of patching it together until finally we reach the "ideal" state which Hegel saw in Napoleon. In the final stage, as in the primary stage, the society is focused in the person of a particular individual. The dominance of Napoleon, however, is regarded by Hegel as a dominance which somehow avoids the suppositions of the original state of history. Napoleon is not the master whose person dominates the slaves; he is the master of free individuals who see their own individuality summed in his individuality. This Hegelian "solution" to history may be misplaced and even theoretically suspect, but I hope that the outline of the dialectic is sufficiently clear—at least up to the point of the final resolution. The dialectic which I have described is, it seems to me, another way of stating what Hegel specifically states as the dialectic of history:

[T]he various grades in the consciousness of freedom—that the Orientals knew only that *one* is free, the Greeks and Romans that *some* are free, while we know that *all* men absolutely, that is, as men are free...offer the natural division of world history and the manner in which we will treat it.[32]

Back, then, to the world historical individual: these culture heroes are those who are able to impress their passion, the concentration of an individuality, onto a society. In the primitive state (which Hegel regards as realized in the Orient) this is quite easy to interpret. In the complex cultures of Europe the dominance of the person of the "master" can never be wholly satisfactory because he is not the sole free man in the society, his persona is not the sole self which is expressed. Nevertheless, insofar as the world historical individual creates these individualizing syntheses, he is the creature of reason, the efficient cause of historical reality. If history is the locus of individuality and self-consciousness; if the *only* possible substance to bear this self-consciousness is a social group; *then* the forcing of a sense of a single self-consciousness onto the society is a profoundly history-making deed. The world historical individual by his personal synthesis of the individual freedoms of the society, his dominance of the political life, creates the social conditions which maximize self-consciousness. In the primitive state his self-consciousness is the measure of the society; in the stage of anti-thesis the ruler may be far from knowing or encompassing his society as a whole. He forces it into a synthesis by his own passion but it is not one he may fully understand: presumably the culture *cannot* be fully comprehended as long as it contains slaves, for it is "irrational." It is the "cunning of Reason" which continuously uses the individualizing passions of the world historical individual to synthesize disparate freedoms into single self-conscious societies.

The source, then, of individuality, of personality in society is the individuality asserted by these political heroes. Societies do not have personalities except as they are made by passionate individuals. These state-makers, however, need not be self-conscious of the society they have made in the fullest sense. The artist may not be able to reflectively discuss or account for the very individual style which we find so revelatory—he may even mis-describe his own work. What is important is that he has the will and talent to create these individualized syntheses. This is what the world historical individual accomplishes: he makes a self-consciousness from his own individual dominance. In the ideal—when Napoleon reads Hegel—he will not only make history (create the synthesis) but understand it reflectively.

In the previous chapter, I discussed the sense in which the final and efficient causes of history are rational for Hegel. The most important single clue for appreciating Hegel's views about the rationality of the historical edifice is the reorientation of our normal view of reason as something which deals with abstractions and universals to the view that reason is the principle both for the construction and the comprehension of individuality. Reason has been linked with such concepts as moral personality, self-consciousness, and individual freedom. From that standpoint, the maker of history—even as passionate—expresses reason as a deeply individualizing act. He creates a spirit for his age, the Zeitgeist, which is a unique, individualized "self-consciousness," in a manner not unlike the way in which an artist creates works marked throughout by an individual stamp. Like the artist, the world historical maker need not be fully rational in the sense of being reflectively self-conscious about his making. He makes, he does not philosophize. Philosophy trails after history as a reflective comprehension of the spirit which it does not create: "The Owl of Minerva always soars at twilight." However, insofar as the hero creates an object with value *as* individual, he accomplishes reason's peculiar task of validating *self*-consciousness. The product of the world historical individual is in its turn something uniquely individual: a people. "It is the absolute interest of Reason that this moral whole [State] exist; and herein lies the justification and merit of heroes who have founded states, no matter how crude."[1] The aim of history, the end of historical making is "the spiritual individual." "The spiritual individual, the people insofar as it is organized in itself, an organic whole, is what we call the State."[2] He adds, "[T]he State is the definite object of world history proper."[3]

If the end and efficient cause of history are rational in Hegel's precise sense of the term, we now turn to examine in what sense the material and formal causes of the "edifice of history" are rational. We ask ourselves, if the aim of the world historical individual is the creation of a rational order, an individualized people, what material will he use to accomplish the end and what form must the creation have. Hegel's answer is that the state is the only proper material for historical making, and the proper form of the state, the constitution, which is finally projected is monarchic. In this section we will deal primarily with the problem of subject matter. A detailed discussion of constitutions is of more interest in strictly political discussion, and I will confine myself to such comments about Hegel's views on the form of states which seem directly relevant to a philosophy of history.

Material and Formal Cause of History: State and Constitution

What is the material in which the final end of reason is to be realized?

> It is first of all the subjective agent itself; human desires, subjectivity in general. In human knowledge and volition, as its material basis, the rational attains existence. We have considered subjective volition with its purpose, namely, the truth of reality, insofar as it is moved by a great world-historical passion. As a subjective will in limited passions it is dependent; it can satisfy its particular desires only within this dependence. But the subjective will has also a substantial life, a reality where it moves in the region of essential being and has the essential itself as the object of its existence. This essential being is the union of the subjective with the rational will; it is the moral whole, the *State*. It is that actuality in which the individual has and enjoys his freedom, but only as knowing, believing and willing the universal.[4]

This passage leads off the section which Hegel's manuscript indicates as "Das Material seiner Verwirklichung." Having noted that the ultimate material in which reason realizes its existence is the individual wills of men, Hegel goes on to locate the more proximate matter of history in the state. The state is not some ontological entity set alongside human will: a count of the things that exist would not include cows, men, and states. The state is an ideal creation, it exists as a framework of human understandings so that, if men ceased to exist, the state would likewise disappear. This point seems obvious, but since some people seem to believe that the state is some sort of superentity in Hegel which has a substantial reality of its own it is important to emphasize that Hegel finds the material existence of reason in individual human beings. On the other hand, the state is an ideal construct. While the state cannot exist except for the wills of men, one cannot *understand* the state by reducing its reality to the actions or desires of individual human beings. Karl Popper, who I have previously noted as an arch-Hegelian critic, espouses a view of historical reality which he calls "methodological individualism." For Popper what really exists are concrete human individuals with their various interests. The state is a "logical fiction" at best. He excoriates conventional history with its records of the doings of states as a record of "international crime and mass murder." If one believes that states are fictions, then wars between states make no sense, they *are* mass murder.[5]

Hegel rejects this reductionist argument. He would admit that the state was an ideal construct, but this does not make it a "fiction" in the negative sense that Popper maintains. If it were not for individual human beings and their desires, there would be no state; for all that, the state is a reality which human beings create that is not in turn reducible to the meaning or status of the original desires. Without certain psychological drives no one would pursue a scientific career, but the "discoveries" or "creations" of that career are not reducible to the meaning of the original drive. Ernest Jones pursues a self-destructive path when he attempts to use Freud's theory of psychoanalysis to discover the psychological origins of the theory. If it is a theory and not a rationalization, then the psychological motivations of the actual human being in whom it was created and sustained are irrelevant. As theory it attains a status which transcends its existential circumstances. So with the state as Hegel views it. Whatever the state is, it cannot be reduced to the subjective conditions which engendered it and in terms of which it maintains actual existence. One could say that, for the scientist, the world of science was the "actuality in which the individual practitioner has and enjoys his freedom [from the limitations of his *personal* existence and circumstance], but only as knowing, believing and willing the universal." In some similar manner individual man as citizen transcends his particularity. Popper wants to deny this transcendence into the "universal" of the state and to insist that only the particular human beings are real. In arguing against Popper's reductionist view, it is also important to see that Hegel is not a reductionist in the opposite direction. Popper and other modern critics of Hegel have the general notion about philosophy that it has as its central task the distinction of appearance and reality. From Popper's standpoint Hegel is a reductionist who thinks that the state is real and the individuals mere appearance. Popper believes that he asserts the proper appearance/reality distinction by making the individuals real and the state appearance. I believe that a fair reading of the passage quoted above would indicate that Hegel simply isn't drawing any appearance/reality distinction at all. State and individual are "real" in different senses, and it is a violation of common sense to try to decide which is the *really* real and then regard the other as *mere* appearance.

In asserting, then, that the state is the only "definite object of world history proper," Hegel is not relegating actual human beings to faint appearances in the march of substantial spirit, as his critics often claim. Nevertheless, there are difficulties with the Hegelian formulation which require explication. We have throughout insisted on the fact that history is interested in individuality. To illustrate what it means to be *interested* in individuality, we have used such illustrations as the interest we have in the individual style of a painter or the interest in self-recognition that occurs in the confrontation of two men in the master/slave relation. The notion of individuals has been tied closely to particular human personalities and their self-consciousness. However, Hegel is most explicit that the individuals in whom history is interested are not particular human beings but the proper historical individuals, states or peoples. Is the extension of the "logic of individuality" to states appropriate? Why is it necessary as Hegel sees it? And is it even clear that Hegel is consistent in speaking of the state as "individual"? What is the meaning of the last sentence in the quotation above which asserts that the state is "that actuality in which the individual has and enjoys his freedom, but only as knowing, believing and willing the universal"? What is the relation between the assertion of the state as the proper historical individual and its role as "the universal" in which the particular human is "absorbed"?

In attempting to indicate the sense in which an ideal construct might have a "transcendent existence" whose meaning went beyond its existential locus in the lives of particular human beings I used the example of "the world of science." I think that there would be no great difficulty interpreting the sentence about individuals and universals if one thought it was a statement about science. The individual scientist is freed from the limitations of his time, place, and person when he participates in the life of reason in science. Insofar as he "knows" and "wills" the universal, he creates and sustains his freedom and the world of science. The triangle which he demonstrates about is not *this* triangle, this particular chalky configuration on this dusty blackboard at this time; it is the universal triangle which may truly exist nowhere but which he and his fellow geometers will into existence and which is the object of their knowledge. If freedom is freedom from the limitations and partialities of *this* existence—either the particular triangle or the particular investigator—then the world of science offers us that freedom. Again, one suspects that Hegelian critics like Popper, who have a primary interest in the logic of natural science, somehow see this model as the one that Hegel is applying to state and individual. As the scientist "sacrifices" his personal existential status for science, in order to gain freedom, so the individual should sacrifice his existence to the state.

I believe that our previous discussions about "the Understanding" would indicate why Hegel cannot have this model in mind for the relation of individual and universal in the quotation. The kind of "universal" which is the object of science is the abstract universal of the understanding, and Hegel repeatedly asserts that the state, while it is "the universal," is the *concrete* universal.

> The universal which appears and becomes known in the State...
> is generally called the *culture* of a nation. The definite content,
> however, which receives the form of universality and is contained
> in the concrete reality of the State is the *spirit of the people.*[6]

The "universal" always has a definite content, and the union comprises the peculiar individuality of a people which, as we pointed out in the discussion of formalism in history, precludes abstract comparisons of the religion, art, and so on of different cultures. Just how one is to give an appropriate elucidation of this "spiritual individual," the state as *concrete* universal, is not easy. Hegel himself struggles for metaphors.

> The state does not exist for the citizens; on the contrary, one
> could say that the state is the end and they are its means. But the

means-end relation is not fitting here. For the state is not the
abstract confronting the citizens; they are parts of it, like
members of an organic body, where no member is an end and
none is means.[7]

This "organic" metaphor won't really do either, though it is one
which Hegel uses frequently. Organic nature can no more serve as a
model for human life in the state, the life of reason and the spirit,
than the mechanical metaphor of means and ends which it rejects.

It is clear that Hegel refers to the state as a "spiritual *individual*"
and that whenever he talks about it as "universal" he immediately
amplifies his claim by asserting that it is absolutely concrete, a
"concrete actuality," wholly determinate and so forth. In this
commentary I have chosen to emphasize the theme of individuality
rather than the notion of the concrete universal. Although both
notions seem to be the same in Hegel, for the purpose of modern
elucidation it seems that the notion of individuality is much to be
preferred. The problem with the notion of concrete universal is that
it is almost impossible for most readers to avoid reading the phrase
within the primary locus of universal as a term of the understanding.
Read from that perspective, concrete universal becomes the notion
of exemplary universal, that is, a concrete universal is an actual
given case, a specimen or an example of a universal. The concrete
universal in that sense is one in which the intelligible character of
the thing lies wholly on the side of the universal and the content
only "fills in" the form. I believe we have said enough already in this
commentary to see why any such formalistic approach must be
rejected by Hegel. The content, the concrete part of the universal, is
as much a part of the intelligibility and value as the "universal."
And this is no additive process in which one must gather the
universal on the one hand and the content on the other; the two are
welded in a single being which must be grasped in a single act of
comprehension. For this reason, then, I have chosen the notion of
individual as the least misleading formulation of Hegel's interest
and have repeatedly illustrated this notion by reference to individual
works of fine art, where something very much like the unique value
and intelligibility of individual style is accepted as a proper model.

Let me, then, put aside the problem of the state as universal,
except in the quite special sense of the concrete universal or
"universal individual," and concentrate on the logic of individuality
as it applies to states. We already know that the individuality which

is the locus of history is no mere metaphysical identification of concrete particulars. (That is the meaning which individuals must have from the standpoint of the abstract universality of the understanding.) When we say that Hegel is interested in individuality as the focus of historical thought, we mean that he is interested in something like differentiated self-consciousness, personality, particular human beings as free, rational beings. If I value my *self*, presumably I value something more than my merely being an instance of some biological or moral essence. It is my uniqueness in my particular existence and history that is asserted. In the case of the objects of fine art, it is something like the unique self-consciousness of Palladio or Picasso that is our final interest. How we might account for this individualizing interest may be a puzzle, but it does appear to exist as something other than the universalizing interests of science. If I assert on Hegel's behalf that history is the locus of this individualizing interest, I may gain some sympathy because of the belief that such an interest exists. However, when one transfers the individualizing interest from its primary location in particular human beings to states and peoples there is likely to be wonder, if not rejection.

To give Hegel's argument for this "transfer" in the most abbreviated and "paradoxical" form: there is no borrowing of the notion of "individual" from individual as person to individual as state; if there is any transfer, it is the other way about. There are only persons, individual self-consciousnesses, because there are individualized states. It is the state which is the primary locus of individuality from which the particular human beings borrow their individual status, not the other way around. It is not individual human personality which is extended analogously to the state; it is the individuality of the state which devolves onto its members. Individual persons do not create the state as person; rather the state has as its end individual persons. The notion of individual value and free, moral, personality is a cultural creation, not a given. Only in certain cultures, the cultures of peoples and states, does the notion of individual human beings come to have a role.

In order to understand this paradoxical reversal, it is necessary to return to Hegel's analysis of the "meaning" of self-consciousness. The notion of reason and individuality, which interests us in history, is concentrated in this concept of self-consciousness, and if we recall how that concept arises in the *Phenomenology* we should notice that it is *necessarily* social. The sense of self-consciousness arises in the confrontation of two human beings; only in this confrontation is the self to be recognized and known. But this language is misleading since it suggests that there is a self already there and the confrontation is just an *occasion* for the recognition of the self. It just *happens* that I come to a sense of my self in confronting the other, but perhaps I might have retired, like Descartes, to my chambers and by taking thought come upon an answer to "what I am." But Hegel says that any self discovered in the mode of Cartesian self-reflection would be as empty and abstract as Descartes' self, which is the empty abstract "I think." The meaning of human self-consciousness as an individual and concrete self-consciousness must come about in an actual, concrete context. Individual self-consciousness, my sense of myself, is not just intellectually discovered in my confrontation with the other, it is *made* in that confrontation.

One need not espouse some difficult existentialist theses about human Being in order to grant plausibility to Hegel's position. Hegel is interested in concrete individuality, something like individual style in the artist. If we ask ourselves in what way does the artist assert self-consciousness, we could well say that it is something he *does*, not something he "intellectually" discovers. I cited above Wolheim's criticism of any view of artistic creation which saw the painting-out as a mere mechanical process for expressing an idea already intuited. He said that such a view was implausible and that "it is even arguable that the accreditation of certain material possibilities as the media of art is bound up with their inherent unpredictability; it is just because these materials present difficulties that can be dealt with only in the actual working of them that they are so suitable for expressive purposes."[8] For Hegel, for history, the point is not merely arguable, it is necessary. There is no real self-consciousness, no concrete self which can be comprehended as a mental image or intuited: what I *am* is continually created in my acts, just as what the artist *is*, is what he does in his works. Expression is not merely a mechanical transfer of a given self into outer reality, it is something which arises only in the confrontation with and mastery of unpredictable materials. In the primary case of self-consciousness, I express and discover myself in the struggle with the freedom of the other person. It is his freedom (unpredictability) which precisely validates him as the medium for my expression of self and which I must master.

Self-consciousness arises in Hegel only in the world of desire.

Intellectual intuition can never know the self because the world of the intellect is a self-less world. Desire posits me as a self in a concrete situation: I am just thus far from the object desired in just this state of need and capability. I am acutely aware in desire of my self as set, limited—*this* being, *this* subject as opposed to *that* object which is what is not-me, which I desire. In that situation, what I am is determined by how the situation is resolved in my action. Is he a coward, a glutton, prudent or rash? we ask, as we understand the situation and wait to see how it will be resolved in action. These personality predicates are validated by deeds accomplished. While this sense of *a* self is initially posited by desiring consciousness, we have already indicated how this is only a sentiment of self, a fleeting sense of being *this* concretely located being, if the desire is given a naturalistic locus. My desire having been aroused by natural objects, I seek to possess them, and on possession my desire is satiated and the sense of self evaporates: having no need, no sense of lack and loss, I return to contentment and imagine myself all-in-all. If I wished to create a permanent sense of self, a funded self-consciousness, I would have to find a situation where possession was always precluded, desire always unsatisfied. Perhaps self-consciousness is the desire of Don Juan yearning after situations of desire. No, that will not do for real self-consciousness, if the desire is for something understood as natural. My *self* is discovered in the character of what I desire; and if what I desire, what I act on, is universal as the objects of nature are "universal," then the extended self is mere boredom and repetition. I exist as self only in the contradictory state of arousing a desire so that I cannot satisfy it. I must wish to possess (the notion of desire) but refuse to possess. (If the dialectic reminds anyone of Kierkegaard's "diary of the seducer" in *Either/Or*, the resemblance is not accidental either on my part or S. K.'s.) The meaning of my desire is deliberately rejected, and I seek to be unsatisfied perpetually. I neither advance nor retreat but remain in perpetual sameness. Again, one cannot create a self in this bizarre manner; one gains only an extended sentiment of self.

To create self-consciousness, I must desire to possess but in a possession which *in itself* is unsatisfactory. The desire which posits the self in the first place is not finally satiated by the act which resolves the relation between self and object. The object still remains exterior, "undigested" even in its possession, and thus my sense of self is extended. And the object possessed must be desired as a self, as something individual and nonnatural, or else my extended self-consciousness is naturalistic and only different in extent, not in kind, from the sentiment of self. The conflict which issues in master/slave is, of course, the confrontation which we are describing. I desire the *self* of the other, the freedom of the other for an act of self-recognition. But in desiring the other's self to create, assert, and discover who I am, I posit an inherently "dialectical" situation. I really cannot "possess" the freedom of the other in the sense of resolving the subject-object dichotomy, because the freedom of the other exists only insofar as the other is other, is free, is *gegenständlich*, over and against me. To kill the other, to make him an animal slave, to reduce him to a tool, would be to deny my initial desire, which was to possess another's freedom. Corpses, animals, and tools lack freedom, so that I can only satisfy my desire for self-recognition by mastery which is no mastery, a possession which is no possession, a slavery which admits the freedom of the slave.

These dialectics of self-consciousness are the stuff of Hegel and his followers down through the contemporary existentialists. I do not wish to sharpen the intricacies any finer than necessary. In general, Hegel could be seen as making the noncontroversial suggestion that human beings only become moral personalities in social situations. Aristotle remarked that he who lives alone is "either a beast or a God." If that is what Hegel is driving at, there might be reasonably wide support for the notion that human beings are essentially social. Hegel is not the only thinker who might argue that the moral valuation of individual human beings is a human social gesture which is not found in the survival of the fittest that marks the world of nature. Many philosophies which emphasize the importance of love insist that man discovers himself in the I-thou relation. What is peculiar to Hegel's analysis is that he asserts not merely the social character of personality but locates that society in the *state*. If the notion of moral personality is a social concept, why can't it be founded on some merely general notion of community, in the bond of love, the family, or, perhaps, social class? The prominent philosophers of the nineteenth and twentieth century who have been impressed by the dialectics of self-consciousness in Hegel have almost universally rejected his view that it was the state which issued from human confrontation. On the contrary, most of them find the state an abstract, bureaucratic, sterile object to be replaced by the true community for self-discovery, family, church, or classless society.

From Hegel's standpoint, the trouble with any of these sug-
gestions is that they would fail to be proper subject matters for
history. They may be proper models for something which transcends
history (or precedes history), but for history only the state will serve
as a proper subject matter. Self-consciousness emerges in the
conflict to possess the freedom of the other. Only that situation
asserts a relation which sustains self-consciousness. It is the
meaning of the conflict and its resolution. Possession of the desired
object is the logic of desire; possession of the other's freedom is the
logic of self-recognition. But this possession can never be appropriately resolved, since no man will allow his freedom to be
possessed willingly (if he did, he would cease to be an interesting
object to the possessor). The resolution is unstable. The coerciveness
of the solution of master/slave marks the unsatisfactory nature of
the relation, yet there seems to be no "appropriate" solution. The
solution is, as we suggested, deeply appropriate for a concrete,
funded self-consciousness over time, but it is the very instability of
the coercion which makes it function at all. If one accepts the notion
that the human confrontation which yields self-consciousness is
unstable and can only be *made* to work, then the state seems to be
the proper designation for this relation.

> The origin of the state is domination on the one hand, instinctive
> obedience on the other. But obedience and force, fear of a ruler,
> is already a connection of wills. Already in primitive states we
> found that the will of the individual does not count, that parti-
> cularity is renounced and the universal is the essential. This unity
> of the universal and the particular is the Idea itself present as the
> State and as such developing itself further.[9]

He says at another place: "The primary distinction to be made [in
the state] is, then, between the governing and the governed."[10] If
master/slave is *the* origin of self-consciousness, then the state is the
natural outcome of the conflict of self-consciousness. The distinction of master/slave, dominance/obedience, governing/governed is
the essence of creating self-consciousness and states.

It would take an argument as long as the *Phenomenology* to
determine finally whether the origin and maintenance of self-
consciousness in the unstable coercive solution of lordship and
bondage is *the* adequate account of the notion of self. I believe the
arguments above indicate a plausibility and follow the contours of
Hegel's argument. The best that I can do here is to suggest why

Hegel rejects other kinds of social solutions to the nature of self-consciousness. One of the solutions which he discusses at length in *Reason in History* is the family. Plato envisioned the Republic as the family grown large, and modern existentialists and theologians have found in the bond of love or the family of God the distinctive mechanism for generating a proper self-consciousness. Hegel comes at the problem of the family through a discussion of the patriarchal state.

> The basis of the patriarchal condition is the family relation.... The patriarchal condition is one of transition, in which the family has already advanced to a race or people. The union has already ceased to be simply a bond of love and confidence and has become one of service. To understand this transition we must first examine the ethical principle of the family. The family is a single person; its members have either, as parents, mutually surrendered their individuality—and consequently their legal relations to one another...or have not yet attained individuality, as children.... They live together in a unity of feeling, love, confidence, and faith in each other. In love, the one individual has the consciousness of himself in the consciousness of the other.... Morality... consists in a feeling, a consciousness, and a will not of the individual personality and its interests but of the common personality.... But this unity is in the case of the family essentially one of feeling, remaining within the limits of the natural... [the] expansion of the family to a patriarchal whole extends beyond the ties of blood relationship, the simple, natural basis of the state. Beyond that the individuals must acquire the status of personality.[11]

For Hegel the family fails to support *historical* consciousness because it does not develop the notion of individuality. We already know when he refers to the bond of family feeling as "natural" that it will fail to offer a principle for history or self-consciousness. In the family the various individuals fuse into a single person which is, in turn, no particular person. If self-consciousness in the concrete sense is to be generated by Hegel, it must be the sense of myself as subject over and against the object. In the family I confront the other in a manner which fuses subject and object, which makes no separation of me and thee. All are one in the common subordination to "the family" as a total unit. In the patriarchal state we begin to have a transition because there is now subordination to somebody, the patriarch. I am acutely sensitive of myself as over and against the patriarch as a self, so that the notion of personality emerges. It is the very mutuality of love in the family which, because it involves no "competition," fails to generate the status of personality and individual self-consciousness.

The very reasons which attract theologians to the family as the ideal community are the very reasons that would lead Hegel to reject it. The family "solves" the dialectics of self-consciousness outlined previously. The freedom of the other is possessed in a manner which is noncoercive and stable. But the very stability of the solution means that the family in its internal concept is historically sterile. The family is held together by natural bonds of feeling, and all its members lose their self-consciousness in that single bond of feeling; the state, on the other hand, must be *made* to hold together. It involves artifice, force, and law because it is an unstable union of free personalities. The state as an artificial creature is created and destroyed by the acts of men out of a sense of their status as free, individual selves. The state, a coercive bond, held together by law, not feeling, has as its basic concept the freedom of each (otherwise the coercion would be unnecessary) and the aim of some*one*, some *few*, *all* to affirm that freedom.

If the peculiar interest of history and historical consciousness is something like individual personality and concrete differentiated selves (as the interest of artistic consciousness is the individual impress on the work of art), then for Hegel this sense of differentiated self-consciousness arises only in the conflict of freedom against freedom. Family or Marxist class are too infected with naturalistic notions to serve as the basis for individualized self-consciousness. If one were to say that the aim of history is to produce an intense, individualized self-consciousness in human beings, then for Hegel it must come through the conflict of selves which occurs in the state as the ancestor of the primitive discovery of self in the conflict leading to master and slave. Historical consciousness is consciousness of the concrete conflict of human freedom—a conflict which properly occurs in the social matrix which is defined by dominance and obedience.

This line of argument links the state to the notion of individual self-consciousness, but it actually inverts Hegel's argument. While it is true that the state does have as its particular aim, in some sense, individual self-consciousness, it would be incorrect to leave the impression that the state is the means to some end of expressing individuality. We know from the text that it is the world historical individuals who are means to the assertion of absolute spirit in the state. As Hegel notes, the use of means-ends terminology is finally inappropriate to discussions of the relation between states and citizens, but still one must affirm the absolute priority of states as the proper object of historical consciousness. It is the state which is the historical *individual*, not the vivid, particular personalities who occur in history.

The reason why Hegel sees the state as the proper historical individual can be discovered by reverting yet again to the master/ slave situation. In the confrontation and resolution which creates self-consciousness, who actually represents attained self-consciousness? Which is the properly individualized, the truly historical consciousness, and thus the historical object? The answer is neither master nor slave. It might appear that it is the ruler who asserts self-consciousness and freedom since he is the master and gets self-recognition, but from Hegel's point of view it is not so. To be sure, it isn't the slave who fails by his surrender to assert human freedom over the natural fear of death. The proper answer is that it is *the situation itself*, the social bond of master/slave which asserts self-consciousness and individuality. If one considers either master or slave alone, then neither has an *attained* self-consciousness. It might appear that the master has an attained self-consciousness, but this is not so.

> The Master's freedom engendered in and by the fight, is an impasse. To realize it, he must make it recognized by a *Slave*, he must transform whoever is to recognize it into a *Slave*. Now, my freedom ceases to be a dream, an illusion, an abstract idea, only to the extent that it is *universally recognized* by those whom I recognize as worthy of recognizing it. And this is precisely what the Master can *never* obtain. His freedom, to be sure, is recognized. Therefore, it is *real*. But it is recognized only by Slaves. Therefore it is insufficient in its reality, it cannot *satisfy* him who realizes it. . . . On the other hand, if—at the start— the Slave's freedom is recognized by no one but himself, if, consequently it is purely *abstract*, it can end in being *realized* and being realized in its *perfection*. For the Slave *recognizes* the human reality and dignity of the Master. Therefore, it is sufficient for him to impose his liberty on the Master in order to attain the definitive Satisfaction that *mutual* recognition gives and thus stop the historical process.[12]

The content of self-consciousness is defined by its object. Since I cannot know myself reflexively in a Cartesian manner—what I know in that reflection is a mere abstract and empty ego—I come to know myself as this concrete self-consciousness by that which is the object of my consciousness. If my consciousness is filled only with objects of natural desires, then I am a brutish, animal self. If the object of my consciousness is other human beings whom I recognize in their rationality and freedom, then my consciousness is free and rational. The master's consciousness is filled with the recognition of slaves, and this recognition does not correspond to the proper concept of human recognition. The slave, on the other hand, has his consciousness filled with the self of the master so that it is in the slave, curiously enough, that the idea of freedom is properly realized. "The truth of the independent consciousness is accordingly the consciousness of the bondsman."[13]

Without further exploration of the intricate versions and reversions of this dialectic, it is sufficient to indicate that neither of the parties actually realizes a concrete, properly *human* self-consciousness. The master's domination exists but is emptied of meaning; the slave sees humanity in the master but does not realize that human self-consciousness in himself since he does remain a slave. Hegel characterizes this relation between master and slave and similar conflicts in social bonds by various coordinate terms: abstract/concrete, universal/particular, objective/subjective. Now one side of the polarity, now the other may be identified with the abstract or the concrete depending on the context of the argument. On the one hand the master's freedom is concrete in the sense that he actually masters the slave, while the slave's sense of freedom is mere idea. But on the other hand, the master's freedom can be shown to be empty and abstract because he fails to see himself in a fully human reality, while the slave's freedom is more real since he has before him the consciousness of the master. I have already indicated that Hegel locates the concept of *individual* as a synthesis of universal and particular, abstract and concrete. As long as the parties in the social bond can be characterized at the poles of abstract/concrete, and the like, then the parties are not realized individuals, are not realized self-consciousness. Each needs the other to complete his reality in the way that the master and slave need one another.

If there is any attained self-consciousness or individualized reality, it is the social bond itself that contains it, since in its various coercive solutions to the polarities of the dialectic this bond approximates the proper notion of self-consciousness. People in various states, according to their roles as masters, slaves, emperors, republicans, philosophes, or bourgeois, realize various *partial* aspects of the fully self-conscious individual. The entire social matrix as the "resolution" of the partial aspects forms a "spiritual individual," a total self-consciousness to which none of the parties of the society ever explicitly arrives. The end of history comes when the polarities are truly resolved and all parties realize the synthesis. The individuals in the society are no longer partial aspects of a spiritual self-consciousness which is implicit in the social bond. The self-consciousness of the individual and the self-consciousness of the society become one, so that there is no opposition between the spirit of the state and the spirit of the individual. The state as spiritual individual—which has been its nature all along—is now mirrored in the realized self-consciousness and individuality of the citizens.

If one follows this line of reasoning about the importance of the state as the "spiritual individual" and hence as the only appropriate subject matter for historical consciousness, then Hegel's views on what I have identified as "formal causality" in history fall into line. The last subsection of (B) in the outline discussed above in chapter 5 is entitled *Seine Wirklichkeit*, "Its [world history's] realization." In that section Hegel discusses constitutions, which he refers to as *Staatsform*.

> Only in the constitution does the abstract entity of the state
> assume life and reality; but this involves a distinction between
> those who command and those who obey. Yet it does not seem to
> be in accordance with freedom to obey, and those who command
> seem to act in opposition to the concept of freedom, the very basis
> of the State.[14]

The existence of a promulgated constitution is a subject which interested Hegel both in his technical and popular writings.[15] It is interesting to note the aspect which he picks out as essential in the constitution: the distinction of rulers and ruled which, he suggests, seems to run against the very notion of freedom which is the basis of the state. In the light of our previous discussion we can see why Hegel thinks a constitution is important and why he singles out the ruler/ruled distinction. The state is founded on a "coerced" solution to the confrontation of human beings in their freedom. There is no natural outcome to this confrontation. The creatures as free are not "natural" creatures, and the mutual recognition of freedom is fraught with almost irresolvable inner tensions. The social bond is an artificial construction, and its very artificial or "coerced" character indicates that a constitution as an extrinsic instrument of governance is necessary. As he says, "If the principle of individual will and consent of all is laid down as the only basis of constitutional freedom, then actually there is no *Constitution*."[16] Were it the case that human beings in their freedom did not conflict, then no laws and rules, no rulers and ruled would be necessary. In the family, the conflict of free individuals is resolved in the natural bond of feeling. This resolution suppresses (or transcends) individual personalities, in Hegel's view. A family which had to regulate the relation of its members by means of stated rules, formal constitutions, and the apparatus of litigation would hardly be regarded as expressing the character of the familial bond. The early Christians in attempting to create a familial bond in the church regarded lawsuits against fellow believers as wholly reprehensible. If one recognizes a multiplicity of free individuals, and not the single "individual" of the family, then some way must be sought to patch together the conflicting freedoms. The tool which is used is the constitution.

A promulgated constitution is, then, the proper form of the life of reason as we have discussed it, because the constitution *realizes*, makes objective the implicit situation of the conflict of freedom which is at the basis of self-consciousness. Hegel thinks that there are only three basic forms of constitution: democratic, aristocratic, and monarchic, and he sees the last as the final and appropriate constitution. "Among these, Monarchy is a constitution in which the others are contained and comprehended as moments."[17] On the face of it this seems curious in terms of his system and hopelessly dated if one wishes to gather any political wisdom from Hegel. It seems contradictory because we know that the dialectic of history is one which begins with the notion that one is free and ends with the realization that all are free. That sounds as if the progress in history should be toward democracy rather than toward monarchy. Hegel distinguishes two kinds of monarchy, however, and it is only a certain kind of monarchy that he projects as the goal of historical progress. As I pointed out in the discussion of Napoleon, Hegel thought that since the aim of history was to develop a self-consciousness and individual freedom, the best society must be one in which the structure of the society expressed individuality.

At the origin of history one man dominates the state, one man is free; he is *the* state and *the* individual. That is. the primitive monarchy in which the ruler/ruled distinction parallels the master/slave relation. In that society the citizen/slave sees individuality and freedom in the person of the king/master. The king is the truth of his consciousness, to use Hegel's phraseology. The "constitution" of the primitive monarchy offers to the citizen the proper object of consciousness, the free human being in the person of the monarch, but the citizen does not realize that freedom for himself. It remains "abstract," an ideal or goal which he seeks to attain implicitly. At the other end of history is the monarchy, in which the citizen recognizes individuality in the person of the ruler, Napoleon, but sees the ruler's freedom as at one with his own. The monarchy which "ends" history expresses the realization of the citizen as a free individual insofar as he sees the constitution summed up in the person of a free individual. The citizen does not look upon the government as a mechanical contrivance because, if he did that, he could not find himself realized in such an abstraction. He looks on individual freedom but a freedom which is at one with his own. In the primitive monarchy the citizen/slave clearly recognizes that the government is the realization of a free individual; in the new monarchy he makes the same recognition, but now he is no longer slave, he is also recognized in his freedom.

I believe it is worth a parenthetical remark about the plausibility in the light of subsequent historical developments of Hegel's projection of monarchy as the constitution of the future. If one takes monarchy in some formal sense: kings, castles, royal blood, and all that, then Hegel could hardly have been more wrong. Royal houses have one by one been eliminated until it seems likely that King Farouk's cynical comment will come true: "In fifty years there will be only five kings left; the four in the pack of cards and the king of England." However, if one gets at the fundamental problem which Hegel is struggling with, then his version of history turns out to be much more plausible than that of such rivals as Marxism. What Hegel claims is that the citizen wants his society to affirm his worth as a person, an individual self-consciousness. If the structure of the state, its constitution, appears to him impersonal, faceless, mechanical, abstract, empty, then he cannot see himself mirrored in that structure. He needs and desires a *person* in whom he can affirm his *person*. The history of much of twentieth-century politics seems to suggest how accurate this view of human society is. If anything, recent politics has been dominated by "the cult of personality," not the triumph of the proletariat or the withering away of the state. From a strictly Hegelian point of view, these modern dictatorships could not be regarded as "advances"; they appear to be atavistic returns to former despotisms where one did not recognize the mutuality of free citizens. Nevertheless, the demand from all sides to get away from "impersonal" government is one which Hegel's philosophy accounts for on the deepest level. Human beings want to believe that their constitution is through and through an edifice planned by persons for persons. The summation of the constitution in the person of a ruler stems from a deep desire to affirm that necessity.

Inevitable Progress: From Potentiality to Actuality

In moving from section B to section C in Hoffmeister's arrangement of Hegel's text on reason and history, we move to yet another Aristotelian consideration. If A is on reason as substance, B on reason and the four causes, C is a consideration of reason as potency and act.

> Historical change, seen abstractly, has long been understood generally as involving a progress toward the better, the more perfect....
> The principle of *development* implies further that it is based on an inner principle, a presupposed potentiality, which brings itself into existence. This formal determination is essentially the Spirit whose scene, property and sphere of realization is world history. It does not flounder about in the external play of accidents. On the contrary it is absolutely determined and firm against them.[18]

In noting the adoption of the Aristotelian language, it is most important, as it was in the previous sections, to indicate where Hegel diverges from Aristotle in his use of these concepts. Aristotle introduces the notion of potentiality and actuality to deal with the problem of the reality of change. Plato, his distinguished mentor, had decreed that only unchanging objects could really be known and could be really real. Aristotle thought that the trick to knowledge of change was to introduce a distinction between the current state of the object as potentially A and its attainment of the actual form when it was fully A. The change of acorn to oak is a process we can *know* because it is movement from potential form to actual form.

If anything, history is a process of change. We saw that this is its most generic categorization in Hegel, so that it is appropriate that he picks up the crucial terminology of his favorite philosopher's analysis of intelligible change. In adopting Aristotelian terminology, however, Hegel cannot simply transfer the central Aristotelian analysis of change to his own work. Aristotle was willing to grant intelligibility to the world of nature but not to history. As he says in the *Poetics*: poetry is more philosophical than history[19] and the reason for the "philosophical" character of poetry is that it has a plot, an inner mode of development which "imitates" the orderly development of nature. The suggestion is very strong in Aristotle that he would not have thought that a philosophy of *history* was possible, precisely because it lacked any plot, any underlying structure of intelligible development. Since Aristotle's basic notion of intelligibility in change was developed to deal with *natural* objects, the use of potency and act terminology must be considerably altered in Hegel's treatment of history.

Hegel's philosophical problem is to develop a "plot" for history, and it is this endeavor which is stated in the doctrine of inevitable progress. It is a doctrine which many critics find empirically false, theoretically impossible, and morally pernicious. The doctrine may prove unacceptable on many grounds, but we should be clear as to the exact character of this "plot." Probably the most common mistake that is made by critics is to confuse Hegel's claims about progressive development as inevitable with the notion of natural necessity: the Aristotelian progress from potency to act in the biological realm. There is no doubt that Hegel invites such misunderstanding with his careless use of biological metaphors in describing historical change. For example: "The spirit of a People is a natural individual [*eine natürliches Individuum*]; as such it blossoms forth, is strong, declines and dies."[20] But, within a few paragraphs, he states his basic, underlying contrast between the world of nature and the world of the spirit to the effect that in the realm of the spirit there is essential change and progress (*wesentlich Fortschrieten*)[21] Whatever the law of progress is, for Hegel it is a *historical* process and cannot be understood as a species of natural necessity. The movement from potency to act cannot be by some kind of internal principle of change similar to the principles which apply in the natural world; that would mean that there was no distinctively *historical* order of intelligibility, the order which Hegel judges to be progressive rather than repetitive.

What kind of inevitability can there be in a changing process which is not natural necessity? What is a *historical* inevitability? Consider an actual discussion of the recent past within the confines of the historical profession. At one time the received wisdom about the American Civil War was that it was an "irrepressible conflict." After World War I a school of historians arose which challenged this thesis and argued that the war was "needless," a conflict produced by blunder and miscalculation. This view, called revisionism, was strongly challenged after the Second World War by such historians as Arthur Schlesinger and Pieter Geyl.[22] The rights and wrongs of the controversy are not at issue here; what is interesting is that the quarrel about the irrepressible ("inevitable") character of the Civil War appears to be regarded by both sides as a proper *historical* argument. This is at least the spirit in which Geyl sums up his discussion with Randall:

> I have not been arguing that the war was inevitable, not even . . . in the ten years preceding the outbreak. I have been arguing that Randall's argument in favor of the opposite contention is unconvincing. The question of evitable or inevitable is one on which, it seems to me, the historian can never form any but an ambivalent opinion. He will now stress other possibilities, then again speak in terms of coherent sequences of causes and effects.[23]

For Geyl, Randall's arguments fail to carry final conviction, and he cites counterevidence. Although it may be immensely difficult ever to decide evitability, still Geyl acts as if this problem was a historian's legitimate task.

There is a sense in which Geyl's argument and the argument against Hegel actually go on in a different plane. If one examines the background of revisionist historians, one discovers that they were very much affected in their reading of the Civil War by their own experience of World War I. In the aftermath of that conflict, it was widely judged that it was entered into through blunder and miscalculation. Wisdom, foresight, and tact could, perhaps, have averted that catastrophe, so it was believed, but it seemed that if one talked of "inevitability" in history it was an invitation to rulers to let destiny take its course and cease to exercise what wisdom they might muster. There was, in short, a moral motivation to revisionist history which rested on a certain view of human beings as free to choose historical outcomes. It seemed that the introduction of "inevitable" scenarios into historical discussions immediately reduced the statesmen to pawns of fate. Critics of Hegel have often made similar judgments. To talk about inevitable outcomes in history downgrades the moral importance of the individual actors and their ability to choose.

If one is immediately persuaded by the seeming contradiction between inevitability and moral freedom, it is interesting to note that the critics of revisionism argue that it is really the revisionists who fail to take the moral issues of the Civil War seriously precisely *because* they deny its inevitability. If one regards the American Civil War as a blundered-into conflict, then Geyl and Schlesinger argue, one diminishes the moral importance of the war. The war was inevitable because of a deep ideological split on the matter of slavery, and if one reconstructs the period so that the war is merely the botched-up product of incompetent leadership, the moral seriousness of the fight over slavery is lost.

I want to emphasize in this brief recounting of the argument that discussions about the "inevitability" of certain outcomes in history need not be regarded as diminishing the moral worth of human action and that some quarrels about inevitable outcomes are ordinary historians' quarrels. Isaiah Berlin has written eloquently on the subject of historical inevitability, but he regards the problem as identical to the traditional theological quarrel about free will and determinism.[24] In Berlin's construction of the doctrine of historical inevitability the doctrine is fallacious and pernicious because it "engenders acquiescence and passive subjection to uncontrollable forces" and reduces the responsibility of individuals.[25] Berlin may be correct in saying that such a doctrine is destructive of the historian's true task, but I do not think it settles the question of *historical* inevitability. In the argument over revisionism those who argue for inevitability (or at least against the revisionist thesis of a repressible conflict) claim that the presence of certain beliefs in American society during the period prior to the outbreak made the conflict irrepressible. Only if the abolitionists or the slaveholders had changed their minds could a conflict have been avoided. This they were in no mood to do, and so the war followed. This pattern of "beliefs" leading to necessary consequences in action is the basic structure of Hegel's notion of inevitability in history. It is because people have certain beliefs about human freedom that certain changes in history are inevitable. To be sure, if the people gave up those beliefs, then different outcomes would result, but Hegel believes that these beliefs are of such a nature that they will not be abandoned. We have already discussed the fact that the state is based upon the belief on the part of all parties that all men are free. The value of the slave to the master is the subjugation of his freedom. If it is the case that the state is based on a tacit recognition of the freedom of its members *but* at the same time is a master/slave form of that recognition, Hegel argues that the society is unstable and will inevitably decay. As long as the underlying belief of society is that all men are truly free, then the course of history must be toward a form of social structure which adequately recognizes and expresses that belief.

Hegel's doctrine of historical inevitability, then, rests upon the same grounds used by Berlin to *deny* the validity of historical inevitability. Berlin wishes to preserve the notion of individual freedom and responsibility while Hegel says that it is the belief in human freedom which is the basic factor in inevitable historical change. To compress Hegel's whole story of history into the briefest compass: once a belief in free individuals arises in human society this belief inevitably determines a certain line of action leading to the realization of that belief in the political structure. The claim can be construed as a historical claim which is no more or less metaphysical than the claim that, once abolitionist beliefs about the evil of slavery became firmly established in the United States, a social and political change was inevitable. One need not pretend to the ability to predict the exact course of the social change—perhaps war was not the only way in which this idea of human freedom might have been realized—but that there would have been a change over time in a definite direction was inevitable unless the belief had been abandoned.

Hegel's notion of historical inevitability is not a theological or metaphysical claim about determinism; in particular, it does not do away with a sense of individual moral responsibility but actually enhances it by making a "belief" in freedom the central force for historical change. What is peculiar about Hegel's view is not its inner logic but its scope. Though, as Geyl suggests, there may be extremely difficult empirical problems in deciding whether the Civil

War was inevitable after 1855, still it seems a sensible question for which evidence can be weighed. The scope of the period is sufficiently limited so the consequences of certain beliefs can be traced with some confidence. But Hegel's claim covers all of history. One might be prepared to say that certain beliefs in India had inevitable consequences in that society, or that beliefs in Prussia had consequences in that society, but can one string all the cultures of man together in a grand march of freedom? Is there some belief, the belief in human individuality, which has really run through the twists and turns of the human past and which has continually put pressure on events in the direction of an "ideal" society in which this belief would be realized? Do all the states of man actually link together as one society in which this belief in individual freedom has been at work? All this seems most grandiose and implausible.

Just how extensive is Hegel's claim? We have emphasized frequently that in terms of the normal understanding of speculative philosophy of history, Hegel's interests are sharply restricted. His interest is confined strictly to *historical* societies, to states, and he does not have to extend the scope of his inquiry to all races and cultures of men. One can be quite specific about the extent of Hegel's investigations. Because he manages to mention all continents and treat extensively China and India, one can fail to notice that his investigation properly begins only with Persia.

> With the Persian Empire we first enter on continuous history. The Persians are the first Historical People; Persia was the first empire that passed away. While China and India remain stationary, and perpetuate a natural vegetative existence even to the present time, this land has been subject to those developments and revolutions which alone manifest a historical condition.[26]

The actual scope, then, of reason in history encompasses Persia, the countries of the Mediterranean basin, and finally northern Europe. The rest of the world is either before history or, like America, yet to be heard from. To be sure, this is sometimes realized by commentators who tax Hegel for his exceedingly parochial view of human history. This is a philosophy of history which a European professor would write! The answer to such a criticism is that in Hegel's judgment history is an invention of the Europeans. Hegel judges that there is a continuity of development within the countries of the Mediterranean area which, through the agency of the medieval church, extends from Rome northward. The claim for a rough "continuity" in this limited geographical and temporal series has some empirical verification. The influences and counterinfluences between these cultures are the stuff of ordinary histories of the West. What interests Hegel particularly is that there is a certain underlying structure of belief in all these societies which differentiates them as a group from African cultures or Asian cultures. This cultural bloc is the historical culture, the group of states which have had as their underlying cultural belief a view which gave reality to historical consciousness. Persia, for instance, is the first historical people partly because it is the first empire which passes away. The very notion of complete dissolution is a historical notion. Cultures whose self-concept is natural may go under, as nature withers in the fall, but they believe that the spring is sure to follow and that the society will revive. From the standpoint of nature, as we have pointed out, the individual dies but the species remains; only when person or culture comes to see itself historically as of value individually do death and destruction become definitive.

In formal outline, then, Hegel's thesis about a progress in freedom sketches out a straightforward historical problem. He claims that certain beliefs have inevitable consequences within a society. This is unexceptionable and is a favorite theme of historians. He then says that a certain basic belief informs a particular bloc of countries. This is an empirical claim which may be verified or refuted by facts. While the task is large, it would not be theoretically impossible. Perhaps he was ill-informed, and one should extend the march of reason to India or restrict it to Greece and after. Finally, the claim that a basic belief has had certain actional consequences in these societies has no deleterious effect on our estimation of the moral worth and free choice of these societies. It is the presence of a moral belief, the belief in human freedom, that is at work in these societies, and the claim that this belief had inevitable consequences is to say that these people took the belief seriously and acted upon it.

Nevertheless, even if one accepts all the aspects of our elucidation of Hegel, he may still feel that this construction does not capture the full flavor of the Hegelian notion of inevitable progress. It may well be that there is a common underlying assumption about human freedom shared by the nations in question and that they may, as a matter of fact, have continually influenced one another from Persia to Prussia, but we can still doubt that there is anything in the record which would constitute progress. What the argument shows, per-haps, is that this large culture has reacted in various ways to the belief in human freedom and that some of the social solutions have been borrowed or traded, but what reason is there to believe that the kaiser in Berlin was that much closer to the ideal than the emperors at Persepolis? Where is the progress?

Thus far, then, I have attempted to offer a construction of "inevitability" in historical discussions which is empirical, not morally destructive, and, as far as I can detect, theoretically defensible. If this is what Hegel means by inevitable consequences in history, that is, necessary outcomes of the belief in human freedom, then there might be a large number of historians and philosophers of history who could accept the notion without qualms. Inevitability in this sense is quite different from natural necessity; it conforms, in fact, to what we often think of as a plot in a work of fiction. In cases of natural necessity the outcome is known completely and in detail, insofar as we are at all interested in it. We know precisely the course of the acorn to the oak and all that we await is its temporal fulfillment. The exact details are ignored because it is the universal form which is the outcome of the process. In the case of plots we do not know the outcome in advance; if we did, sitting at a play would be extremely boring. What we see in the end of a well-plotted story is that, given certain factors at work, the outcome was inevitable. If not, then it was a bad plot. Appreciating inevitability at the conclusion of the story does not at all mean that we could have predicted the outcome—again, unless it was a trite story. However, if one accepts this notion of inevitable outcomes in history, a non-naturalistic interpretation of the movement from potentiality to actuality, one need not by any means accept the doctrine of inevitable progress as Hegel outlines it. A much more plausible and widely held philosophy of historical change would be to accept the factors which Hegel places into the historical story but to say that history illustrates a perpetual struggle over human freedom. To be sure, the belief in human freedom has deeply affected various cultures—perhaps just those cultures which Hegel is interested in—but what we finally get are a series of noble attempts and tragic failures to stabilize these beliefs into an acceptable social structure. Sometimes there has been progress, sometimes decline. Free so-cieties can count on no inner law of progress to shore them up, they must be continuously renewed in the resolution of each generation. The notion of a progress from Persia to Prussia fails to emerge.

There is no denying the fact that the rise and fall of great states and empires is a distinctive feature of the historical world which Hegel surveys. Sheep grazed on the Acropolis while Hegel was lecturing in Berlin on the progress of reason. Why doesn't Hegel adopt a philosophy of history which would view these multiple cultures as so many progresses toward an ideal state; each with its own inner triumphs and tragedies, each finally destined to decay while the struggle is renewed again in some distant barbaric corner of the dying empire? In fact, he often seems to come close to accepting such a view. History is, after all, the stage on which many great individual peoples have flourished with their own noncomparable inner life and then vanished.

> There are in world history several large periods which have passed away without further development. Their whole enormous gain of culture has been annihilated and, unfortunately, one had to start all over again from the beginning in order to reach again one of the levels of culture which had been reached long ago—assisted perhaps, by some ruins saved from the old treasure—with a new, immeasurable effort of power and time, of crime and suffering. On the other hand, there are continuing developments, structures and systems of culture in particular spheres, rich in kind and well developed in every direction. The merely formal view of development can give preference neither to one course nor the other; nor can it account for the purpose of that decline of older periods. It must consider such events, and in particular such reversals, as external accidents.[27]

The first view sketched out is often stated as the final wisdom about human cultures. The second may seem more controversial, but one could regard specialized areas such as scientific culture as having some kind of rough developmental continuity through their many vicissitudes. In the passage Hegel suggests that he finds the weak point to be in the theory of cultural decay. What is the principle for the decay of past cultures?

In answering that question there are only three possibilities as far as Hegel is concerned: chance, nature, and history. We have discussed these three choices at length in chapter 3; now let us see how they apply to the current problem. There are a number of problems which would plague a theory which alleged that the decay of states was due to chance. In the first place, it just doesn't appear to be true. To be sure, we think that early Minoan civilization was so devastated by the eruption at Thira that it never recovered, but sheer bad luck of that kind seems to play a small part in the fall of states. The witticism that if Cleopatra's nose had been an inch longer history would have been profoundly altered, is just a witticism because the forces at work in Rome and Egypt at that time were such that the queen's physiognomy offers only a grace note on events. Historians just don't give over decline and fall to chance, they persist in looking for the dry rot in the seats of power, the inability of technology to master new challenges, misallocation of resources, failure of nerve, and so on. Except for devastating catastrophe, they look for some inner forces within the society which caused its decline.

A second problem with chance as the explanation of the decay of past states is that it suggests a curiously unhistorical attitude toward these cultures. If it were just chance that the Greek city-state disappeared, then its reintroduction at a later stage in history could be contemplated with equanimity. Because there was nothing inherent in the model which leads to dissolution its revival can be properly undertaken. This would be like regarding the Greek constitution in the manner of Greek mathematics. The latter may suffer eclipse by ill fortune (the caliph burns the library), but the chance which obscured these truths may equally revive them whole and intact. One picks up the story of mathematics without a hitch, as if it had never been interrupted, and the conversation with Euclid goes forward. We have said enough about Hegel's views of the individuality of cultures to indicate how fundamentally he would oppose any such view of cultural renaissance. Products of the understanding, transcendent universal concepts can be easily revived because they are essentially unhistorical; but states and their constitutions are idiosyncratic products of certain concrete conditions, and they cannot be reconstructed.

> The constitutions wherein world-historical peoples have reached
> their flowering are peculiar to them, hence give no universally
> valid basis.... It is different with science and art. The philosophy
> of the ancients, for example, is so much the basis of modern
> philosophy that it must be contained in the latter as a fundament.
> The relation here is one of uninterrupted development of an
> identical structure, whose foundations, walls and roof are still
> the same. In art, that of the Greeks is the highest model. But
> in respect to the constitution it is different; here the old and new
> do not have the essential principle in common.... [N]othing is so

inappropriate as to use as models for our constitutional institutions examples from Greece, Rome or the Orient.[28]

Hegel thinks that the decline of states has to be viewed more profoundly than as the ill-chance of fortune. Whatever leads to their demise is an inner principle, and it is an inner principle so enmeshed with the particularity of their whole cultural expression that they could not—at least as states—be reconstituted.

If there is an inner principle of decay in societies, and we can relegate chance to a minor role at best, then we cannot, of course, accept the view that the principle of decay is natural. There is no natural necessity for states to decay for, if that were the case, Hegel's entire central thesis about the difference between historical objects and things of nature would be destroyed. Biological models of birth and death such as are favored by Spengler or Toynbee are anathema to Hegel as principles for history. It is doubtful that many historians would be happy with the notion of natural necessity operating as an internal principle for the destruction of cultures. That is inevitability in the bad sense. However, there is a mixed theory which is often adopted that sounds very plausible and would account for the facts of growth and decay. This theory would see all cultures as a struggle between history and nature; between culture and inner barbarism. Freud's view of culture would support such a philosophy of history. Human life is, for Freud, a struggle between civilization and its discontents; between reason and the anarchic forces of the libido.

> The fateful question of the human species seems to me to be whether and to what extent the cultural process developed in it will succeed in mastering the derangements of communal life caused by the human instinct of aggression and self-destruction.[29]

History is a kind of Manichean struggle between nature and civilization; now one is in the ascendant, now the other. Nature remains savagely caged in the heart of civilization, waiting to come forth in a rage of destruction and conquest. This dualistic theory is very attractive. It offers an explanation for what appears to be one of the most notable parts of the historical record, the rise and fall of states; at the same time, it validates the importance of human reason and civilization. It seems to call forth a moral effort on the part of humankind to maintain the values so painfully gained.

From Hegel's point of view this dualistic theory of the rise and fall of cultures is both too optimistic and too pessimistic. It is too optimistic because it seems to rest on the assumption that civilization as such is in good shape if only it could really subdue the forces of nature. As a matter of fact, it cannot, so the struggle is eternal. For Hegel the trouble with past civilizations has been a defect in the civilization as such, not a mere unhappy inability to manage natural passions. From Hegel's standpoint, it is the very gestures of reason and freedom that are the culture creators which carry with them the seeds of destruction. Civilizations destroy themselves in terms of *inner* contradictions. The theory is too pessimistic since it can never really see any hope for curing the defects of civilization—the defects come from the inevitable natural background of civilized living. For Hegel, because the problems of past civilizations have been through and through distinctively human problems having to do with rational choices, it is possible actually to improve upon the past, to learn from the past and to "progress."

In the Aristotelian terms used in this commentary, the fault in the Freudian theory of cultural decay is that the efficient cause is nature, while for Hegel the efficient cause is historical consciousness. Reason is the efficient cause of the creation *and* the destruction of states. Insofar as the world historical individual is the destroyer of culture, for example, Caesar of republican Rome, the conflict could be regarded as one between passion and law. For Hegel, however, the passion of the world historical individual is not Freud's libidinal passions which are "outside the realm of history"; it is the peculiar passion of individuality which reduces the old cultural patterns to mere material for a new individualized synthesis. If the force which destroys culture is indeed reason as individualized self-consciousness, then Hegel has laid the groundwork for his belief in progress. Each destruction incorporates the destroyed culture because the destruction is a destruction by and through culture. Nature does not preserve cultures, it is the deadly enemy of the discontents of civilization. But the culture destroyer in Hegel's view sees in the object he overcomes at least a partial reflection of the drive which leads him to destroy. Just as the master in overcoming the slave, the basic historical overcoming, preserves the slave, valuing his freedom because it is the only way that he can accomplish his aim as master, so the culture destroyer subdues culture from motives which are at one with the essence of the civilization. As the old culture expressed human freedom in its institutions, so the new culture seeks the same.

Hegel's theory of progress is not easy to accept or to elucidate. Its strongest points are its emphasis on the through and through historical character of past civilizations and the structure that it offers for "learning" from the past. If the lesson of the past is that cultures decay from chance or undigested nature, then there is little we can learn from those cultures about how to preserve human freedom. If the state may be overthrown by chance or an eruption of natural passion, then we can be wary, but the inroads made by these forces on the previous culture remain as mere external forces to its inner rationale. As a *culture* it was fine, except that a volcano did it in or it failed to do what, after all, can't really be done anyhow— subdue natural passion. For Hegel it was the culture itself which was defective because it failed to find a constitutional expression for human freedom. It affirmed that one or some were free but could not see how to affirm that all were free in a concrete polity. Its failure as a civilization places it historically, it cannot be revived, but its failure is immensely instructive. The culture decayed because it instantiated a belief in individual freedom but failed to actualize it adequately, and so it was inevitable that it would decay. The fundamental belief in freedom spread throughout the masters and their slaves is the efficient cause of cultural change. When the old cultural expression is destroyed, it is destroyed by the belief in freedom which seeks yet a better expression in the new culture. All other cultural destruction is irrelevant to the interest of history, which is just this tracing of the development of political freedom. The old culture is not just tossed aside by external forces, by boredom with the way things are; it is discarded because of the realization, however inchoate, that the old ways of expressing a society of human freedom were a *definitive* failure. One of the reasons we cannot revive these past constitutions is because they are definitive failures.

But if past cultures contained inner contradiction and hence were destined to fail, why can't we learn from the past and simply create the ideal state without waiting out the tedious and destructive turns of the historical record? Because if there is to be any movement toward an ideal, it must come about historically. In our discussion of Condorcet's views about the progress of the human mind, we pointed out the fundamental difference between Hegel's views on the progress of freedom and that of the Enlightenment. While it is true in a formal sense that man's nature is free for both thinkers, in Hegel this means that the content of man's life is for him to create. That man is free means for him that man is peculiarly historical, he must work out his vision of himself by a series of concrete experiments and projections. In the thought of the Enlightenment, man is essentially nonhistorical, and the actual historical record is in itself of no real value in coming to know the true nature of man—that we know via an ahistorical intuition, and our job is simply to make the actual world match the ideal world. Hegel believes that man is essentially historical and that he lacks any intuition of his ideal self: he only gains that vision through the painful process recorded in history. This means, then, that the story of man's freedom could not have started full-blown by some happy accident of genius, fate, or fortune. There could not have been some ideal state in Eden or Athens from which man has somehow strayed into the despotisms of history. If an ideal state is to be made at all, it must come as the end product of historical experience. Anything less is to deny the essentially historical character of humanity. The ideal state is not something that we could know over and above our experience in history. The ideal state is the place of pure rationality, the home of the rational man par excellence, but Hegel does not believe, as the Enlightenment thinkers did, that the notion of rational man has any determinate content discoverable by means other than the actual workings of history. We know the content of rational man by seeing what men have actually done; just as I know what kind of an artist I am from seeing what I actually manage to produce, not from the sketches and ideals in my head. Thus, if the ideal state is even feasible, it is feasible only through a historical education of mankind; it could not have been realized at an earlier time any more than one could now predict the character of painting in the first decade of the twenty-first century. This position of Hegel's is the basis for his "conservative" political bias. The conservative does not believe that history proceeds by leaps; progress does not come about when finally an exasperated humanity lets some moral or philosophical genius rearrange society in the proper rational fashion. Progress truly is the work of history.

The Lessons of History

"What experience and history teach is that peoples and governments have never yet learned from history, let alone acted according to its lessons."[1] This may well be the most-quoted apothegm in all of Hegel—it is also likely to be the most widely misunderstood. It is usually quoted to make a sour observation bearing on the ignorance and indolence of political leaders—as compared, perhaps, to historians. It is often paired with Santayana's quote: "Those who do not know about history are bound to repeat it." The context of Hegel's remark gives the appropriate interpretation, however. The next sentence reads: "Every age has conditions of its own and is an individual situation; decisions must and can be made only within, and in accordance with, the age itself."[2] If this is paired with Santayana's aphorism, nothing could express a more profoundly un-Hegelian view of history. The one thing that Hegel is sure of is that history never repeats itself, so that a man who scours history for the pattern of the present is in profound confusion about the character of historical reality. The burden of this commentary has been to insist that history is concerned with the individuality of *historical* reality; one should never expect the past to give lessons to the present. In this last chapter I wish briefly to suggest in some large and rather loose ways what the real lessons of the past are for Hegel. In so doing I will be attempting to suggest what the lessons of Hegel's philosophy of history are.

Reason in History: A Summation

The central quotation for this entire commentary was the one on reason as the Lord of history, in which reason was identified as the substance of history, its material, formal, efficient, and final cause, working itself from potentiality to actuality in the course of time.

The main sections of the commentary attempted to elucidate that claim by exploring the particular use which Hegel makes of the notion of reason. Reason has been explicated by a string of inter-related notions: human freedom, personality, self-consciousness, individuality, the concrete universal. The constant temptation of the unwitting interpreter is to read into Hegel a doctrine of the understanding which is wholly incapable of validating historical reality. The understanding is the world of nature, the universal, the general, the abstract, the merely formal. If the understanding exhausts the field of what is known and intelligible, then history as such disappears since the objects of history disappear. History finally values the individual as such, and not as an instance or a case, as with the understanding. Hegel introduces "the categories of Reason" into history because, without such categories, there would be no basis for regarding individuals as either interesting or intelligible. To be sure, the understanding "knows" that there are concrete existents, but their *concreteness* is irrelevant to their intelligible character as universals. If historical reality is to have any value and intelligibility, one must validate individuality in its concreteness. This, Hegel believes, is what historians normally do even though they might be hard pressed—by philosophers like Hempel—to give an account of why the concrete record is of value as such. To find historical reality, one must look at the world rationally—and then the world looks rationally back. It looks rationally back because the only "objects" which have individualized value are human beings. It is not, of course, as biological specimens of *homo sapiens* that they emerge as having individual value. Man as a rational being, which Hegel interprets as a being with self-consciousness, turns out to be an object which, insofar as it asserts its rationality and self-consciousness, creates and sustains something which is both individual and intelligible. Reason, then, is the substance of historical reality. Only the products of reason can be given individual value, only they have historical consciousness and can be the object of a historian's investigation.

Reason creates a nonnatural world which declares its nonnatural character by the very fact of individual value. Human self-con-sciousness is a cultural product of human beings, it is not part of their "natural" character. Human beings cannot be *self*-conscious except in certain social conditions, and it is self-consciousness which is the proper object of history. Not all human societies create and sustain individuality or self-consciousness. The family is a human community in which individual self-consciousness is not affirmed, where individuality is melded into a common consciousness of the whole. The family lies "outside of history" because it does not provide objects for historical interest. Self-consciousness is created in those social groupings which Hegel labels "states." For Hegel, the state is the peculiar locus of the individual because it involves a distinction between ruler and ruled. Only in such social situations does the problem of individual freedom arise and assert itself. Since self-consciousness is a social creation, involving complex relations of dependence and independence, many social situations fail to assert full self-consciousness, full affirmation of rationality and freedom in the parties of the society. It is not the particular members of the society that constitute an individual, free, self-integrated, and self-conscious entity: it is the society as the resolution of the partial freedom and self-consciousness of the members that is undivided, a whole individual. Insofar as history is rational reality, the reality of something individual and free, it is the state which emerges as "the spiritual individual" and as the proper locus of historical consciousness, the proper object for the historian's interest.

Reason, then, creates the spiritual individual in the form of the state because, in the state, particular human beings realize a kind of self-consciousness and affirmation of their individual worth and freedom. As particulars they may lack full self-consciousness to the extent that the structure of the state is unable to resolve successfully the tensions between the freedom of ruler and ruled—a distinction which is, at the same time, necessary, if there is to be self-consciousness at all. The meaning of their freedom is beyond them in the total life of the state; it is not something that they can fully realize as particulars. This creation of reason, the state, proves therefore to be subject to continuous instability. Reason appears in self-contradiction because it seeks to realize the freedom of all in a structure which requires "masters and slaves." History is a search for a solution to the internal dilemma of political life; it is a search for a resolution of the conflict between the rulers and the ruled, the state and the citizen. What is desired is a society in which the citizen realizes in his particular being the individuality and self-consciousness which is patched together in the state as a whole. And, of course, if that state could be achieved, the patching would cease to be subject to destruction. Hegel judges that this search for a social order which would allow individual human beings to enjoy full self-consciousness is not chimerical. Since reason initiates the process, it could not have embarked on an "irrational" task. In creating individual self-consciousness in the first place, reason was dealing only with its own inner complexities. The situation which produces self-consciousness is not a conflict between reason and some alien force it cannot master, it is the conflict of reason with itself. Self-consciousness arises not in a contrast with alien nature but in a confrontation between two rational beings both of whom affirm their rationality and their individual worth, albeit in an imperfect manner. The dilemmas which beset societies and lead to their disruption and new cultural forms are problems which reason sets for itself.

The turnover of states and peoples, the record of history, is not then a mere aimless turnover of cultural groups. All cultures aim at the bringing of the particulars (citizens) into full freedom and self-consciousness. They are created for that purpose, and they are destroyed in an attempt to improve the culture in the light of that purpose. Nor can one regard the cultures of the past as so many "experiments" in freedom—as if reason proceeded like a chemist trying different formulas until finally he "hit upon" the right solution. That view would undermine the very importance of the whole historical record, the actual achieved individualities of the past. If the central thesis of reason in history is that individuals, spiritual individuals, have a value *as* individual, then one could hardly accept the notion of history as "experiments in freedom." In the case of the experiments in freedom, the actual achievement of the "right answer" would be a result of mere luck or doggedness *or* because one knew what the answer would be ahead of time. The "ideal state" could be realized any time some culture got an inspiration and hit on the proper formula, or when it finally divined by some deep meditation just the proper kind of society and proceeded to bring it into existence. If one held that view of the ideal state, then all the other states of history would be just so many unhappy mistakes which, with luck, grace, or a perfected political philosophy, could have been avoided. Not so for Hegel: the historical record is irreplaceable; nothing can or will shortcut the way to a solution of the problem reason poses for itself. Only history can produce the perfection of history; only the actual historical cultures can lead on to self-consciousness and reason.

History, then, involves "inevitable progress." Reason creates states to establish itself as self-consciousness, but many of the forms established prove to be imperfect versions of the inner concept of self-consciousness and mutual recognition of freedom. "The object does not correspond to its notion." Each culture has the *aim* of expressing mutuality of freedom. We refuse to accept the notion that reason sets itself a problem which it cannot solve. "Human reason has the peculiar fate that in one species of its knowledge it is burdened by questions which, as prescribed by the very nature of reason itself, it is not able to ignore, but which, as transcending all its powers, it is also unable to answer" (the first sentence of *The Critique of Pure Reason*). Not at all, says Hegel. There is no factor which Hegel will admit that *necessarily* frustrates the rational aim. The ideal state is possible. Having set out to create and perfect self-consciousness, reason does not leave that perfection to chance. Reason is "both substance and infinite power." The ideal is not only a possible notion, it is also something that reason alone can and must realize. Reason creates history and historical consciousness, and it is in and through history that the ideal is realized. History must be reason operating as "its own exclusive supposition and absolutely final purpose, and [working]...out this purpose from potentiality into actuality, from inward source to outward appearance." There are no other acceptable alternatives.

Either reason sets itself a problem it cannot solve or, if it can be solved, then it must be solved by the very objects, means, forms, which reason creates. Those objects are the individuals of history. The ideal cannot be posed by reason but brought into existence by chance or grace, by prophet or philosophe. What would it be like to pose a mathematical problem which could not be solved by mathematical means but depended on some chance event or a divine revelation? Prophet and philosophe fail as makers of the ideal because their state is derived from transcendent, ahistorical revelation or cogitation. The prophet and the philosophe lack historical consciousness since they know only the universalized patterns of either nature or super-nature. One cannot find self-consciousness in transcendent, universal forms. Any ideal revealed in prophecy or excogitated from philosophical principle must be inadequate in its fundamental concept to the problem of self-consciousness. If there is to be a means to the solution of reason's search for self-consciousness, it must come *through* self-consciousness, which is what is lacking in the utopian schemes of the savant.

Reason "valorizes" individuality-historical consciousness, and it does so because it judges there is a value in fully attained self-consciousness. A sense of self-consciousness can only be obtained by a sense of other self-consciousnesses. I come to know who I am as an individual by placing myself in respect to other selves, their lives, their styles, their human worlds. I can sense my individuality only by ranging it alongside other individualities. Reason's production of multiple individualities enriches my self-consciousness. These cultures become means for my self-comprehension. Even if history does not progress, it continually should enrich our sense of self as we gather the nuances of our world in comparing it to other individualities. But, finally, reason is not simply interested in an indefinitely enriched self-consciousness, for this would ignore the real failures of individual states in the past to synthesize effectively the particular as citizen and the state. To be sure, past cultures are individuals to be understood only as such, but the attained individuality can be scaled against the ideal individuality. Other individualities not only enrich, they have a progressive tendency which is more than merely quantitative.

Reason and the Historian: World Philosophical History

Reason creates history, it creates historical consciousness, it creates a human world, a second "nature" for man which contrasts sharply with nature as the realm of species. World philosophical history is the investigation of reason as historical consciousness. It is the history of historical consciousness. Historical consciousness is purposive: it seeks to establish self-consciousness and the ideal state—the same end seen from different aspects. It is reason which in conferring worth on individuality, the concrete (universal), makes the study of history sui generis, a unique manner of understanding. The existence of individuality creates a world with a certain inner logic which cannot be understood on the model of the world of mathematics or physics. The problem of historical knowledge is to comprehend individuality *as such*, to make individuality intelligible without reducing the individual to the inarticulate particular or the universal form. How can this be possible? I believe that we can arrive at a final insight on world philosophical history by returning again to two accepted models for history—history of art and history of science—which in certain ways incorporate the insights which Hegel insists must go into any real historical investigation. In a sense the two fields are the subjective and objective poles of history that must finally be synthesized in a proper appreciation of historical consciousness.

The relationship between "knowing" an art object and the history of art, between "connoisseurship" and the objects of past production, offers striking parallels to some of Hegel's views about history in general. A connoisseur interested in understanding and evaluating a particular painter's style is very much in the same position as the Hegelian historian following the injunction of self-knowledge. (An even more precise analogy would be a painter interested in understanding his own style, but this is less frequent. Painters paint and critics reflect.) There is a very strong presumption that the best way of knowing this *particular* style is by comparison and contrast with the styles of other painters. It also seems to be the case that the broader and more detailed the knowledge of actual art historical achievements, the finer the sense of discrimination about the individual characteristics of this painter being examined. There is no natural limit to the field of artifacts which the art historian-connoisseur will consider except the empirical totality of what has been produced. At one time it might have seemed absurd to think that one could be aided in evaluating European easel painting by examining African masks, but Picasso changed that. In turn, one can argue that every new work or style enriches our sense of the already extant. Picasso's neoclassical works sharpen our sense of Greek forms and vice versa.

The resemblance to Hegel's views are clear. In the first place, the focus of interest is clearly something individual. We want to know just what constitutes Cézanne's style. Knowing this individual style cannot be regarded as some sort of subsumption under a species or a universal style. We really know very little about individual style in being told that Cézanne was a "postimpressionist." If knowing an individual style such as Cézanne's were like knowing this individual item as a triangle, then one could have people painting Cézanne paintings who were not Cézanne. In the case of works of scientific understanding, one can literally continue the work of an Einstein or Newton. There is nothing individual about the theory which makes it peculiarly Newtonian; the name is attached *honoris causa.* In the case of works of art one cannot continue Cézanne's painting or Keats's poetry. To be sure, people imitate their work or write in the manner of a master. Sometimes it may even be very difficult to discern the work of the ardent disciple from the master. Nevertheless, there is a deep-lying belief that finally individual nuance will assert itself and even a super Van Meergen will be seen clearly as a fraud.

Secondly, appreciation of an individual style comes about because we can discriminate *this* man's work from the work of others. There is no substitute for awareness of the actual achievements of others. If we remember the comments about the problems of "formalism" in art, it is clear that only "in the presence of the actual work of art" do we understand what critical language is about. One could not, in short, devise a list of descriptive adjectives, no matter how fine-grained which would shortcut the need to experience a variety of actual styles in coming to an assessment of the particular work at hand. In the case of general history, one could not derive a law or theory which would serve to explain or understand the current *individual* problem. A general theory of revolution, for instance, derived from historical cases, would not finally yield an understanding of *this* revolution. Kenneth Clark can write a book about "the nude" as a style in painting and trace a variety of interesting relationships and traditions, but no generalities about the painting of the nude can predict the character of the individual object. We are helped only by fitting this particular work into the actual chain of works from Phidias to Renoir. In short, nothing substitutes for *historical* awareness, acquaintance with the actual empirical examples, in assessing individual style. The lack of general rules for appreciation and assessment fits with Hegel's insistence that history cannot be regarded as a form of theoretical knowing. In the case of art appreciation, the lack of such theoretical understanding has, in fact, led those imbued with the scientific model to regard the work of the connoisseur as merely intuitive, subjective, a knack at best, but surely not a kind of knowledge.

For philosophers, there is an almost perfect parallel to the way in which art critics reach insight on a particular case with Wittgenstein's general philosophical method. Wittgenstein felt that the way in which we could gain perspective on a particular language muddle was to surround it by cases all varying from the original case in slight ways. This method of procedure was accompanied with a stern injunction against any attempt to derive general *rules* about usage. If there were general rules, then the assembly of cases could certainly be dispensed with and we could appeal directly to the rule. What we are searching for is insight into the particular through the gathering of other particulars, and we rule out mediation through a universal (a rule).

If one says that the aim of history is self-consciousness, then the analogy from the history of art seems fruitful. One can make a plausible case that one knows one's own "style" better in terms of every contrast and comparison made to the individual styles of the present and the past. Every achievement contributes to a clearer sense of our own particularity, if only by a nuance. (The importance of nuance in artistic evaluation should not be underrated. What appears "all the same" to the untutored viewer becomes a rich field of very important individual difference to the connoisseur.) One can offer a plausible view that some similar process is at work in general history except that it is not artistic "style" that we are interested in but a whole range of styles, political, artistic, scientific, religious, which in Hegel's mind finally coalesce in an overall style which defines a particular age or culture. To know ourselves or our culture we must range it alongside these other styles. In this manner we avoid cultural parochialism and arrive at a more "universal" vision.

This line of argument would certainly justify the notion that historical studies must finally be crowned by a *world* history—the common hope, as we pointed out, of many nineteenth-century historians. In the search for self-understanding the whole range of actual human achievement makes that self-concept richer and more precise. But, if one develops this model for Hegelian history from the analogy offered from the history of art, one is likely to make a fatal mistake, at least in terms of "normal" understandings of the history of art. As we noted, the normal understanding of the history of art would be what Hegel regarded as "subjective." History of art is a form of *Spezialgeschichte* in which the accomplishments are linked together "merely [by an] external thread" and they lack an "internal guiding soul." The subjective model supports a certain kind of quest for self-consciousness but not Hegel's quest.

History of art as normally conceived on the subjective model is essentially nonprogressive (in this we contrasted it with the history of science), and as a result "every epoch is equally close to God." We pointed out that from Hegel's point of view such a model finally lacked historical consciousness. But before abandoning the art historical model, we must emphasize how it accentuates certain aspects which Hegel believes are absolutely essential for world philosophical history and which can easily be lost in a "progressive" model for history. A nonprogressive, "subjective" history cannot impose any "objective" value upon its subject matter—like "truth" in the case of history of science—and so every age is accepted with equanimity in terms of its own kinds of expression. The subjective model fully justifies the world historical perspective, since in understanding my artistic style I will profit from the contrast I can make with ancient art and the cave drawings. Progressive, objective history, on the other hand, such as the history of science, is always in danger of defeating its own program. If contemporary science is the true picture, what profit is there, really, in going over the oddities and falsities of the past? Science seems always in danger of forgetting its history and starting off de novo from discovered truths. Art critics feel that the history of painting is essential to understanding present work as a certain kind of self-expression; scientists seldom feel that the appreciation of current results benefits from awareness of Archimedes or Dalton.

I have already made a case in chapter 2 for understanding Hegelian history on the model of history of science in order to bring out the progressive and "objective" character of Hegelian history. The analogy offered from the history of art runs counter to that earlier argument. Haskell Fain in an excellent analysis of Hegel has also pointed out the close relation between Hegel's way of understanding history and the conventional philosophy of the history of science.[3] But, as he says, if that is what Hegelian history is all about, it produces a story of man, not a history. History of science usually tells us the *story* of physics—how one intellectual discovery was succeeded by another, correcting, altering, overturning, or revolutionizing the past practice—with the *history* of physics dropping to a mere shadow. The times and places, the circumstances and conditions of scientific discovery—most of what we think of as historical data—are really of small importance in showing how a science moved from one intellectual construct to another. Fain says that Hegel's fault as a philosopher of *history* is precisely that he neglected history in favor of an intellectual story. Although Fain goes on to argue that historians do need stories after all and one should give Hegel credit for realizing that, nevertheless, if Fain's argument holds, Hegel's method for constructing general history would be seriously defective. If Fain is correct, the analogy offered above from the history of art would also seem to be inappropriate for Hegelian history. One might sum up this dilemma in Fain's terms by saying that history of science has all story and no history, while history of art is all history and no story.

We can pose the problem in Hegelian terminology by asking which of two models from conventional history is the more appropriate paradigm of "philosophical world history"—history of art or history of science, subjective or objective history? The history of art model emphasizes the empirical irreplaceability of actual historical achievement and the antijudgmental, antitranscendental side of Hegel's philosophy of history; the history of science model contains the progressivist and therefore objectifying strains which would account for Hegel's own animadversions on the past. One can guess that a Hegelian answer must somehow synthesize both aspects, combining "subjective" and "objective" in a unique method.

If we look at the two paradigms, both fail to capture in the fullest degree a "sense of history." History of art requires history in the sense that the actual, empirical, individual achievements of various artists and styles are indispensable in coming to understand a present style; there is no transcendent rule which supervenes over the assemblage of cases. One moves "immediately" from concrete case to concrete case, and only by this direct juxtaposition does one gain insight into the case at hand. While this paradigm saves the empirical, it subtly undermines a common feature of what we regard as history. Would it make any difference to the appreciation of the individual style in question if all the various artifacts considered had been produced in the past five years (or five minutes) by legions of artisans? Even though it could hardly have happened that way, in actual assessments of individual style, one could fairly say, all artifacts are treated as contemporary. The antiquity of oriental style is not a factor in discussing the influence of Japanese prints on Van Gogh. One could say that art lacks a story in the sense that one does not need to place event before event to construct a proper thread of understanding. To be sure, one must do this minimally, in the sense that Japanese prints had to exist *before* they could influence Van Gogh, but how far before, how they happened to be shown in Paris at that time, what their historical provenance was is irrelevant in comparing the two styles. Even this minimalist condition can be dispensed with if our interest is sharply confined to understanding the individuality of a style. It is useful to compare Dürer's woodcuts with Hokusai though there exists no historical connection. If "philosophical world history" were conceived on the model of history of art and we emphasized that it aims at self-consciousness, then the actual historical placing of peoples and civilizations would become very secondary. The antiquity of Rome does not interest us as such in comparing its "style" to our own. In fact, there are numerous "histories" produced on these models which make immediate comparison between America and the Rome of the Caesars, Germany and the Age of Pericles, as if these were contemporary styles to be admired, vilified, or even chosen. "Philosophical world history," understood on the model suggested, would preserve lovingly the empirical detail of the past but would ignore its pastness, its *historical* dimension.

In the case of history of science the situation is the reverse. There we have a definitive "narrative" sequence in the sense that it is illogical to place Einstein before Newton or the atomic theory before phlogiston. Some kind of linear placing is forced on history of science by the actual contents of the scientific achievements. The achievements of science make a direct, internal comment on other achievements. This is not generally thought to be the case in the history of art, and it is this distinction of external and internal relation between the various moments of the histories that constitutes the difference between subjective and objective history of ideas. The trouble with the linear placing which marks the history of science is that it is not essentially a *historical* placing. If we imagined a situation similar to the one above where we fancied all works of art had been produced by hordes of craftsmen in the last five years, in the case of science there would be a marked difference. One might imagine the atomic theory emerging from an intensive weekend seminar, and if someone were to write a history of the conference he would order the various proposals in terms of the ways they contributed to the final "true" answer. He might note times when the eminent savants wandered into unfruitful areas or offered theories which were subsequently shown to be wrong, but the governing order would be a kind of step-by-step building up to the "answer." The historical time sequence is subordinated to the logical sequence of how the theory was constructed. The story of the atomic theory may in fact have taken ages or an afternoon seminar, but as story it can remain the same. Unlike the history of art model, history of science does construct a simulacrum of pastness. Hegel is keen to say that ancient Greece is historically placed and cannot be a model for present action. In history of science the "logical" rejection of earlier theories by present theories assures that they remain dead, past, no longer possible options. If Hegel modeled philosophical world history on history of science as we have constructed it, he could certainly retain the sequential character which we think of as part of the notion of history, but the sequence would be "logical" not historical. The beliefs of ancient Greece are past because they are definitively overcome by present beliefs in the manner in which the ether has disappeared permanently from discussions in physics.

Is there a resolution of these subjective and objective models? Philosophical world history cannot be construed as either history of art or history of science writ large—at least in the models we have outlined. Philosophical world history in the terms of this discussion could be characterized as "the story of history." But doesn't the *story* of history mean that we will take the empirical stuff out of the past and refashion human cultures on a logical, not a historical, scale? This is certainly what Fain thinks Hegel is about. But this opinion fails to dig deeply enough into the meaning of the story of *history*. Fain notes that for Hegel the story of history is the story of freedom, and he thinks that is not an unworthy candidate for the story of history. However, for Hegel the relation between "history" and "freedom" is analytic while for Fain it is regarded as "synthetic." "History as the story of freedom" is logically equivalent in Hegel to "history as the story of history." If history is the story of some ahistorical concept, the march of democracy, the search for truth, the quest for love, then one can virtually ignore the historical embeddedness of these journeys and reconstruct the sequence along the "logical" steps toward this "transcendent" goal. History is not the story of freedom in that sense for Hegel. Freedom is not a transcendent goal which can be defined ahistorically and in terms of which the actual record of the past can be seen to measure up or not. This would make "freedom" a moralistic term and convert actual history into a series of examples in the manner of formalist historians. In Fain's analysis, the *story* of x is neutral as to historical character, so that when Hegel, as he rightly says, attempts the story of freedom, he must be doing something which is only tangentially historical. However, if one says that the formula is "the story of history itself," it is difficult to see how it can be only tangentially related to history.

In order to understand the formula for philosophical world history one must appreciate one of the repeated points of this analysis, namely, that "history" is a value-descriptive term. When Hegel talks about "history" he is pointing to a certain *kind* of event or sequence of events which is discriminated from the sense of "history" as all datable events. In Hegel's sense, "the story of history" functions *somewhat* like "the story of truth" in describing the history of science. There is a sense in which "history" points to a "transcendental" value which is realized within datable sequences. History as value descriptive "transcends" the totality of events in the sense that only certain kinds of events possess the quality of historicity. One could say that "historicity" was a transcendent or a priori concept which is applied to events and that these events are instances of that concept. But, this concept of historicity in its *content* functions in precisely the opposite way to "normal" concepts which belong to the categories of the understanding. The purpose of normal concepts is to abstract from the individuality of the object conceived and to categorize them generically. When I categorize an object as historical I utilize the categories of reason, which means that in these events I am directed to pay attention to the individuality as the important and revelatory aspect. Broadly put, I have before my gaze all space-time events (what might be thought of as the total "historical" field). Hegel says, in effect, "Now there are two ways to view this field. Some of these events are natural events and there you will be interested in the repeated patterns which present themselves *in* particular cases. The other manner is historical and there you will be interested in the unique, individuality of the item examined. As a matter of fact, you will discover that only certain objects, rational beings, offer any interest on the side of individuality and the picture of the doings of these rational beings is uniquely and essentially historical."

"The story of history," then, is a tale which recounts how human beings came to regard their *history* as having any value; it is the story of self-consciousness, freedom and reason. It differs from the history of art model in the important respect that not all human doings are on a par in terms of the respect paid to individuality and freedom. Hegel's own treatment of the art of various countries illustrates this point. All art expresses a cultural style (or a personal style), and in that sense we can come to know our own style better by comparison and contrast, but for Hegel not all art forms express the fullness of self-consciousness. To take one of his most notorious examples, he sees the Egyptian Sphinx as the cultural expression of humanity not yet emancipated from nature, that is, not really individualized and historical. Greek art of the golden age, on the other hand, expresses an interest in the individual and the autonomy of man from nature. In comparing the two styles we do not simply get an insight into different modes of self-consciousness, we also get a *story* of self-consciousness in which the latter style "rejects" the earlier because of a higher spiritual content. To be sure, this kind of analysis is not much appreciated in contemporary accounts of art. From Hegel's point of view that would demonstrate the inadequate "subjectivity" of history of art. There is a kind of false catholicity of taste which fails to see that certain forms of art *as* cultural expression reflect an inadequate if not immoral concept of humanity. Nazi art is a defined style and one could learn something about other styles by regarding its "accomplishments," but the image of man which it sets forth is as debased as the political philosophy which supported it.

The story of history, then, sees a "progressive" realization of the value of historical consciousness and a rejection of inadequate visions as options wholly past and dead. There is a story to the value-descriptive notion of history because various human events have an internal connectedness such that certain cultures negate the imperfect historical consciousness of the past. Why this relation also happens to be progressive in a rough fashion across time is perhaps no more difficult to understand than why history of science is progressive. As a "matter of fact" science has progressed, and Hegel would think that empirical data would indicate the same in the progressive realization of human freedom. But one suspects that there is something more to this progress in both cases than mere happenstance. Somehow the notion of scientific truth or of belief in the value of the individual, once let loose on the world, impels a kind of progress however wayward and diverted.

There can be a story to history, then, because various cultures as expressions of historical consciousness are not related just as so many equal options and styles but in an internal manner which forces the negation of one culture by another in a manner analogous to the negations in the history of science. Thus, Hegel's "censorious" manner in treating various cultures. In the story of history these cultures are failures in certain ways because they lack the values attached to historical consciousness. But if there is a story to history, one must emphasize that this is the story of *history* which is not a "transcendent" value in the manner of "truth" in the story of science. If history is analytically related to freedom and self-consciousness, then the story must conform to those categories. When we affirm the importance of a *historical* approach we are saying that the actual, empirical, individual achievements are irreplaceable by any generic characterizations. History as the story of freedom says that rational, free beings are of value as individuals; or, to say the same thing, their actual history is instructive qua history, not as an example or type. The history of science as we have outlined it conforms to Hegel's categories of the understanding. Those who practice it are ahistorically positioned. History of science could be written anonymously because it is the truths which are related to one another, not the scientists. The history of history cannot be written anonymously because it is the series of achievements of historical entities, that is, individuals as concrete entities. Because the story of history is the story of unique value attached to free beings it cannot be predicted ahead of time any more than one can predict new styles in art. One waits to see what individual insight will achieve. At the same time, however, it is the story of free beings, and Hegel believes that one thing that history will not show is a trend submerging freedom and respect for individuality.

In sum, then, philosophical world history is: (a) philosophical because it is a story, there is an internal relatedness between the events; (b) it is world history because it profits from all the actual achievements of men, which are irreplaceable in discriminate self-comprehension; (c) it is history because it has a story (it is not just a series of cross-cultural comparisons) and it has a history (it regards actual, empirical deeds as irreplaceable). There are many works which pass under the title of history which Hegel would regard as essentially lacking in a sense of history. The moralist who regards history as a series of examples uses historical materials in a fundamentally nonhistorical manner. Our modern "realism" quickly rejects such moralizing histories. At the same time a "subjectivist" approach to history, which is often allied to the rejection of moral evaluations, converts the past into a field of different "styles" in which the importance of historical position and our moral interest in history is downgraded. Certain ways of finding a story in history in the light of transcendent values progressively realized convert historical position into logical antecedent and consequent. Hegel's complex "method" attempts to retain the irreplaceability of the empirical and the individual without removing the notion of direction or position in history—what counts in the story.

History is the discipline of the moral connoisseur. If we try to split that notion apart, we fail to get history or the lesson of history. Moralists fail to get the lesson of history because they have an a priori concept of man—human rationality, the proper human self. When they look at the past they use it in an exemplary fashion to illustrate a moral; they do not learn from the history. Connoisseurs only pay attention to the actual historical achievement, it is the measure of what man is and can be; we await the new genius to tell us the limits of art. But the connoisseur finally fails to get any lesson from history. For him it is an infinitely rich compendium of styles and cultures which illuminates the present but does not finally offer a basis for evaluation and judgment. In attempting to understand history as at once empirical and a priori, individualized and yet leading to some achieved value, Hegel offers a scheme of comprehension which is often extremely difficult to comprehend; but, then, historical consciousness may be much deeper and more profound than one would first imagine.

Notes

1. Introduction

1. Hegel, *Reason in History,* trans. R. Hartman (Indianapolis, Ind.: Bobbs-Merrill, 1959). Hereafter cited as Hartman.

2. Hegel, *The Philosophy of History,* trans. J. Sibree, (New York: Dover Publications, 1956). Hereafter cited as Sibree.

3. Sibree, Introduction to the Dover Edition, unpaginated.

4. Jean Hyppolite, *Introduction à la Philosophie de l'Histoire de Hegel,* (Paris: Librarie Marcel Riviere, 1948). Since writing this Introduction, I have learned that an old friend and colleague, Burleigh Wilkins, has a book forthcoming from Cornell University Press on Hegel's philosophy of history. I hope the scholarly world can bear two works on Hegelian history after such a long drought.

5. Hegel, *Die Vernunft in der Geschichte,* ed. Johannes Hoffmeister (Hamburg: Felix Meiner, 1955). Hereafter cited as Hoffmeister.

6. Hegel, *Vorlesungen über die Philosophie der Geschichte,* ed. Theodor Litt (Stuttgart: Philipp Reclam, 1961). Hereafter cited as Litt.

7. For an account of the textual problems see Hoffmeister, p. 272 ff.

8. Hegel, *The Philosophy of Hegel,* ed. Carl J. Friedrich (New York: Modern Library, 1953), lv-lvi. One commentator who makes a great point of the difference between manuscript and notes is Walter Kaufmann. Kaufmann is a highly literary person and so his interest in the ipse dixit of the Master may have some point. I have not been able to discern any *philosophical* difference between what is said in the notes and in the manuscript, and if Kaufmann has seen them he has not as yet told us what they are. Kaufmann is right, no doubt, to urge caution, but I believe I am following the scholarly tradition in regarding the notes as generally reliable.

9. Hegel, *The Phenomenology of Mind,* trans. J. B. Baillie (London: Allen and Unwin, 1931). Hereafter cited as *Phenomenology.*

10. Jean Hyppolite, *Genèse et Structure de la Phenomenologie de l'Esprit* (Paris: Aubier, 1946). Alexandre Kojève, *Introduction à la Lecture de Hegel* (Paris: Gallimard, 1947). This latter work has been partially translated into English, A. Kojève, *Introduction to the Reading of Hegel,* ed. Allan Bloom, trans J. H. Nichols, Jr. (New York: Basic Books, 1969). Citations from the English translation are cited as Kojève.

11. Hegel: *A Collection of Critical Essays,* ed. Alasdair MacIntyre (Garden City, N.Y.: Doubleday, 1972), p. 219.

12. Ibid.

13. The only work by title in the field is Arnold Hauser, *Philosophy of Art History* (London: Routledge and Kegan Paul, 1959).

2. *Does Hegel Have a Philosophy of History?*

1. W. H. Walsh, *Philosophy of History:An Introduction* (New York: Harper, 1960). The volume was first published in London under the title *An Introduction to Philosophy of History*, in 1951, which is a fair date from which to mark the revival of interest in philosophy of history among analytic philosophers.

2. Ibid., p. 12.

3. Ibid., p. 14.

4. Ibid., p. 15.

5. William H. Dray, *Philosophy of History* (Englewood Cliffs, N.J.: Prentice-Hall, 1964), p. 1. Dray notes that the distinction may not be all-inclusive and cites E. L. Fackenheim's *Metaphysics and Historicity* (Milwaukee: Marquette University Press, 1961). Fackenheim's views are related to the position stated in this commentary.

6. A. Donagan and B. Donagan, *Philosophy of History* (New York: Macmillan, 1965), p. 1.

7. "Contemporary philosophers of history, with good reason, generally write with one eye on the neighboring field of philosophy of science" (Dray, *Philosophy of History*, p. 1). Dray points out that there is really no speculative philosophy of science, or cosmology, as this kind of enterprise is "somewhat out of fashion" (p. 2). Walsh makes a similar appeal to a parallel distinction in philosophy of science (Walsh, *Philosophy of History*, p. 15).

8. Carnap's major statement is *The Logical Syntax of Language* (New York: Routledge and Kegan Paul, 1937). For his later reply to his critics, who claimed that logic of science could not be done without ontological assumptions, see Carnap, "Empiricism, Semantics, and Ontology," *Revue internationale de philosophie* (1950): 208–28. Much of the controversy stems from lack of clarity about the role of "metaphysics," which is sometimes seen as a continuation of science (or history) by new and unacceptable methods, sometimes as a reflective study of the "ontological" grounds of science which does not compete with actual empirical research.

9. Hoffmeister, p. 164; Hartman, p. 75.

10. Hoffmeister, pp. 164–65; Hartman, p. 76.

11. Donagan and Donagan, *Philosophy of History*, p. 1; Walsh, *Philosophy of History*, p. 14. I do not wish to deny that Hegel is interested in a kind of "universal" history, but it is the totality of historical actions, not the "totality of past human actions."

12. Quoted in Herbert Butterfield, *Man on His Past* (Cambridge: Cambridge University Press, 1955), p. 2.

13. R. G. Collingwood, *The Idea of History* (Oxford: Oxford University Press, 1946), p. 257 and passim.

14. These phrases tend to be used interchangeably, and it is not always possible from the English text to know what the German is. I prefer "philosophical world history," or "the philosophical method of historical writing," because they have fewer connotations of speculative "philosophy of history."

15. Die dritte Gattung der Geschichte, die philosophische Weltgeschichte knüpft sich an diese letzte Art der reflektierenden Geschichtsbetrachtung so an..." (Hoffmeister, p. 22).

16. "Der allgemeine Gesichtspunkt der philosophischen Weltgeschichte ist nicht abstrakt allgemein, sondern konkret und schlechtin gegenwärtig..." (ibid.).

17. Hoffmeister, p. 4; Hartman, p. 3.

18. Hoffmeister, p. 10; Hartman, p. 6. Hartman has this statement under the heading of universal history, but it appears in Hoffmeister's text as part of the general introduction to reflective history.

19. Hoffmeister, p. 31; Hartman, p. 13.

20. Hoffmeister, p. 20; Hartman, p. 9. Hartman notes that the German is ambiguous in spots, but his translation expresses what Hegel must have had in mind. The parenthetical remark on Niebuhr would confirm Hartman's reading.

21. Hoffmeister, p. 20.

22. Collingwood, *The Idea of History,* p. 130.

23. Hoffmeister, p. 9; Hartman, p. 5.

24. For documents and appraisals of the Beard-Becker thesis, see Hans Meyerhoff, *The Philosophy of History in Our Time* (Garden City, N.Y.: Doubleday, 1959).

25. For example, *The Reconstruction of American History,* ed. John Higham (New York: Harper, 1962).

26. The problem of what the historian knows "indirectly" is a basic ambiguity in the account of "original history." Ideally, one might regard the scope of the original historian as unlimited since anything might be regarded as indirectly known, for example, by reports of other historians dealing with earlier ages, and so on ad infinitum. It is a measure of the naiveté (not in any pejorative sense) of the original historian that he confines his scope to very immediate sources of information. If one were to do a full-blown phenomenology of historical consciousness in the manner of *The Phenomenology of Mind,* it would be necessary to point out the "contradictions," that is, arbitrary limitations, within the earlier stages which drive consciousness on to more and more inclusive and reflective levels.

27. Hoffmeister, p. 11; Hartman, p. 6.

28. I am not making the claim which Toynbee makes in the opening sections of *A Study of History* (New York: Oxford University Press, 1962), particularly on page 17, that partial views of history are necessarily false. I am only alleging that once the expansion is begun from original history there is something arbitrary about choosing a line of demarcation. Hegel would regard this partiality as "false" but not in Toynbee's sense. The concept of history "demands" universal history, and partial histories are false to that idea but not false in themselves.

29. The ideal of a universal history—world history—was regarded by the German historical school as a necessity for completing historical research. This continued to be Ranke's great dream and exercised nineteenth-century historians down through Acton. See the account of this in Butterfield, *Man on His Past.*

30. Hoffmeister, p. 12; Hartman, p. 6.

31. Ibid.

32. Hoffmeister, p. 17; Hartman, p. 7.

33. John Dewey, in *Logic: The Theory of Inquiry* as excerpted in Meyerhoff, *Philosophy of History,* p. 166.

34. Ibid., pp. 167-68.

35. Hoffmeister, p. 20; Hartman, pp. 8-9.

36. In Carl Becker, *Everyman His Own Historian: Essays on History and Politics* (New York: F. S. Croft & Co., 1935).

37. Hoffmeister, p. 21; Hartman, p. 9.

38. "Auch dies ist eine Art, Gegenwart in die Vergangenheit zu bringen..." (Hoffmeister, p. 21).

39. "If we can never remove the subjective element from our narratives [by the study of the history of historiography], we can neutralize it somewhat by realizing how men are conditioned.... It is through the neglect of this self-discipline that in one age after another history operates to confirm the prevailing fallacies and ratify the favourite errors of the time" (Butterfield, *Man on His Past*, p. 23).

40. Hoffmeister, p. 21; Hartman, p. 9.

41. There are, of course, Marxist and Freudian reductionists who might claim that any idea that exists in a subject is no more than an existential pressure peculiar to the subject. Such a view would regard history of science as the history of subjective opinion. The defects in such views are manifold and will not be argued here.

42. Hoffmeister, p. 28; Hartman, p. 11.

43. Mircea Eliade, *Cosmos and History* (New York: Harper, 1959).

44. In the case of political ideas "objectification" obviously involves more than proving that certain political theories are true about man; it involves the "objectifying" of those ideas in concrete political institutions. The difference between the two types of "objectifying" is crucial to a proper understanding of Hegel's philosophy of the historical. When a scientist tests a theory, he regards an instance as a type which proves his case; the objectifying movement of proper history is toward something peculiarly *individual* which cannot be understood as an instance of a type. The nature of this difference is the main burden of this interpretation of Hegel and is dealt with extensively in later chapters.

45. Hoffmeister, p. 80; Hartman, p. 27.

46. Hoffmeister, p. 4; Hartman, p. 3.

3. Objective Reason

1. Hoffmeister, p. 25; Hartman, p. 10. As noted, in the Karl Hegel edition from which Hartman's translation stems, this material from the Second Outline is incorporated as part of the final paragraph on the philosophical method of writing history from the First Outline.

2. Ibid.

3. Hoffmeister, p. 26.

4. Ibid.

5. Ibid.

6. Ibid.

7. Hempel's classic statement, "The Function of General Laws in History," is reprinted in P. Gardiner, ed., *Theories of History* (Glencoe, Illinois: Free Press, 1959), pp. 344-56.

8. Alan Donagan, "Historical Explanation: the Popper-Hempel Thesis Reconsidered," *History and Theory*, 4 (1964-65): 3-26.

9. Hoffmeister, p. 174; Hartman, p. 85.

10. *Phenomenology*, p. 808.

11. Hoffmeister, p. 28; Hartman, p. 11.

12. G. R. G. Mure, *An Introduction to Hegel* (Oxford: Oxford University Press, 1940); *A Study of Hegel's Logic* (Oxford: Oxford University Press, 1950).

13. Hoffmeister, p. 49; Hartman, p. 19.

14. Hartman, p. 12; Litt, p. 50.

15. Hoffmeister, p. 29.

16. ". . . nature is a source or cause of being moved and of being at rest in that to which it belongs primarily, in virtue of itself and not in virtue of a concommitant attribute" (*Physics* 2. 1. 192b 22 [Oxford translation]).

17. Hoffmeister, p. 37; Hartman, p. 13. The Anaxagoras passage is at the end of Section A in Hoffmeister's text, which in general is much expanded from the Karl Hegel version because of the reordering of materials which appear at later parts of this version.

18. Hoffmeister, p. 34; Hartman, p. 88.

19. Hoffmeister, p. 35-36; Hartman, p. 88-89.

20. Hoffmeister, p. 149; Hartman, p. 68.

21. Karl Popper, "Prediction and Prophecy in the Social Sciences," in Gardiner, *Theories of History*, p. 279.

22. Sibree, p. 87.

23. Hoffmeister, p. 36.

24. Sibree, p. 457.

25. Hegel, *Early Theological Writings*, trans. T. M. Knox (Chicago: University of Chicago Press, 1948).

26. The complications of Hegel's relation to Christian orthodoxy are illustrated by considering Karl Löwith's *Meaning in History* (Chicago: University of Chicago Press, 1949). Löwith's book denies that from a Christian point of view there is any meaning *in* history. The meaning of human existence is found in a transcendent dimension, not in any immanent process. Insofar as Hegel really looks for a meaning *in* history he would fail to be theologically oriented and thus Löwith (a Christian) and Kojève (a Marxist) might both agree that Hegel's theory was basically a-theistic. Thus, Hegel's affirmation of a close relation between providence and his own view is not ipso facto proof of any religious demands on the reader. If providence is immanent meaning in history, Löwith, at least, would regard Hegel's philosophy of history as quite secular.

27. Hoffmeister, p. 38; Hartman, p. 14.

28. Hoffmeister, p. 40; Hartman, p. 15.

29. Litt, p. 54.

30. Hoffmeister, p. 40.

31. *Phenomenology*, Section A, 1.

32. *Phenomenology*, p. 790.

33. Kant, *Critique of Pure Reason*, trans. N. K. Smith (London: Macmillan, 1950) A216, B263: "By nature, in the empirical sense, we understand the connection of appearances as regards their existence according to necessary rules, that is, according to laws."

34. Conversely, if Kant with his view of nature has trouble with freedom, Aristotle with his view of nature has no trouble with human responsibility. For the Greek it is only common sense that some events in a man's life come about by nature (puberty),

some from art (dental repair), some by training (skill in gymnastics), some by learning (skill in mathematics). If actions stem from a man's character, they are his and he is responsible for them. Aristotle has been much criticized for failing to deal with the problem of freedom, but I share John Austin's opinion that this criticism is unjust (see J. L. Austin, *Philosophical Papers*, ed. J. O. Urmson and G. J. Warnock [Oxford: Oxford University Press, 1961], p. 128).

35. J. N. Findlay, *Hegel: A Re-examination* (London: Allen and Unwin, 1958), p. 21.

36. Hoffmeister, pp. 153-54.

37. Hegel, *Philosophy of Nature*, ed. and trans. M. J. Petry (London: Allen and Unwin, 1970), p. 212.

38. Hoffmeister, p. 151; Hartman, p. 69.

4. Subjective Reason

1. Hoffmeister, p. 31; Hartman, p. 13.

2. Hoffmeister, pp. 32-33.

3. Ibid.

4. Ibid.

5. Findlay, *Hegel*, p. 60.

6. *Phenomenology* A, III, contains an extended discussion of *Verstand*.

7. Sibree, pp. 64-65; Litt, p. 119; Hoffmeister, pp. 168-69; Hartman, p. 80.

8. Hoffmeister, pp. 169-70; Hartman, p. 81.

9. Hoffmeister, p. 172; Hartman, p. 83.

10. Hoffmeister, p. 174; Hartman, p. 85.

11. A. Isenberg, "Perception, Meaning and the Subject Matter of Art," in *The Problems of Aesthetics*, ed. E. Vivas and M. Krieger (New York: Rinehart, 1958).

12. Ibid., p. 219.

13. Hoffmeister, pp. 30-31.

14. *Phenomenology*, p. 196.

15. Ibid., p. 197.

16. Donagan, "Historical Explanation," p. 15.

17. Bertrand Russell, "The Philosophy of Logical Atomism," in *Logic and Knowledge: Essays 1901-1950*, ed. R. C. Marsh (London: Allen & Unwin, 1956).

18. Kojève, p. 73.

19. Findlay, *Hegel*, p. 90.

20. Kojève, p. 3.

21. *Phenomenology*, p. 220.

22. Kojève, p. 4. The subsequent account of master and slave relies heavily on Kojève; see especially pp. 3-30.

23. *Phenomenology*, pp. 272-73.

5. Reason in History—I

1. Kojève, pp. 32-33.

2. Hoffmeister, p. v.

3. Hoffmeister, p. 110; Hartman, p. 49.

4. Hoffmeister, p. 138.

5. Hoffmeister, p. 63; Hartman, p. 25. This is Hartman's translation from the Karl Hegel text which is, in turn, a compressed form of the similar passage in Hoffmeister.

6. Hoffmeister, p. 78; Hartman, p. 26; Litt, p. 62.

7. Hoffmeister, p. 63; Hartman, pp. 24-25.

8. Sibree, p. 457.

9. Kojève argues in several places that the prime failure in Hegel's system is the ultimate confusion between nature and spirit. Kojève's general line of interpretation is one which ignores Hegel's various attempts at a synthesis of the two in the absolute, and he firmly believes that the substantive results of Hegel's phenomenological analysis of human beings as essentially historical remain. In general, I agree with Kojève's point that for an analysis of historicity one can and should ignore the various attempts to overcome the dichotomy of nature and spirit. At the same time, Kojève is writing out of an existentialist milieu which is more willing to proclaim a final "absurdity" to human, that is, individual historical existence in the face of nature. Individuality is truly *de trop* as far as nature is concerned. Hegel would surely have found such "absurdity" unacceptable, and the "solution" would be a Lord of nature and history, if such a being could be conceived. A faith in history may carry theological consequences, but it surely goes against common sense to insist on a theological deduction of the possibility of history before tackling the archives.

10. Hoffmeister, p. 50; Hartman, p. 20.

11. Condorcet, *Sketch for an Historical Picture of the Progress of the Human Mind*, trans. J. Barraclough (London: Methuen, 1955).

12. R. Wollheim, *Art and Its Objects* (Harmondsworth: Penguin, 1970), p. 58.

13. Hoffmeister, p. 105; Hartman, p. 44.

14. Hoffmeister, p. 51; Hartman, p. 21.

15. Hartman, p. 21.

16. Hoffmeister, p. 51.

17. A problem which a latter-day "Hegelian," John Dewey, points out with great effect in *The Public and Its Problems* (New York: Holt, 1927).

18. Hoffmeister, p. 54.

19. Hoffmeister, pp. 78-79; Hartman, p. 26.

20. Ibid.

21. Ibid.

22. Hoffmeister, p. 105; Hartman, p. 43.

23. Hoffmeister, p. 85; Hartman, p. 29.

24. Ibid.

25. Hoffmeister, p. 93; Hartman, p. 36.

26. Kant, *Idea of a Universal History from a Cosmopolitan Point of View*, in Gardiner, ed., *Theories of History*.

27. Hoffmeister, p. 83; Hartman, p. 29.

28. Hoffmeister, p. 110; Hartman, p. 49.

29. Kojève, p. 69.

30. Hoffmeister, p. 109; Hartman, p. 48.

31. A notable recent critic is E. H. Gombrich, *In Search of Cultural History* (Oxford: 1969). Gombrich criticizes Burckhardt as a Hegelian. Since art history is a field in which stylistic periods have been accepted and fruitful notions, the animad-

versions of this distinguished and perceptive theoretician of art are particularly interesting.

32. Hoffmeister, p. 62; Hartman, p. 24.

6. Reason in History—II

1. Hoffmeister, p. 112; Hartman, p. 50.
2. Hoffmeister, p. 114; Hartman, p. 51.
3. Hoffmeister, p. 115; Hartman, p. 53.
4. Hoffmeister, pp. 110-11; Hartman, p. 49.
5. Popper, *The Open Society and Its Enemies*, excerpted in Meyerhoff, *Philosophy of History*, p. 305.
6. Hoffmeister, p. 115; Hartman, p. 51.
7. Hoffmeister, p. 112; Hartman, p. 52.
8. Wollheim, *Art and Its Objects*.
9. Hoffmeister, p. 146; Hartman, p. 60.
10. Hoffmeister, p. 139; Hartman, p. 58.
11. Hoffmeister, pp. 118-19; Hartman, pp. 55-56.
12. Kojève, p. 50.
13. *Phenomenology*, p. 237.
14. Hoffmeister, p. 139; Hartman, p. 57.
15. Hegel, *Political Writings*, trans. T. M. Knox (London: Oxford University Press, 1964).
16. Hoffmeister, p. 138; Hartman, p. 57.
17. Hoffmeister, p. 142.
18. Hoffmeister, pp. 149, 151; Hartman, pp. 68-69.
19. Aristotle, *Poetics*, 1451g5.
20. Hoffmeister, p. 67.
21. Hoffmeister, p. 70.
22. A discussion of the history of the history of the Civil War can be found in Higham, *Reconstruction of American History*, chap. 6.
23. Pieter Geyl, *Debates with Historians* (Hague: Martinus Nijoff, 1955), p. 235.
24. Isaiah Berlin, "Historical Inevitability," in Meyerhoff, *Philosophy of History*, p. 249.
25. This is Geyl's summation of Berlin's argument. Geyl, *Debates with Historians*, p. 240.
26. Sibree, p. 173.
27. Hoffmeister, p. 152; Hartman, p. 70.
28. Hoffmeister, p. 143; Hartman, p. 61.
29. S. Freud,*Civilization and Its Discontents* (Garden City: Doubleday, 1958), p. 105.

7. The Lessons of History

1. Hoffmeister, p. 19; Hartman, p. 8.
2. Ibid.
3. Haskell Fain, *Between Philosophy and History* (Princeton: Princeton University Press, 1971).

Index

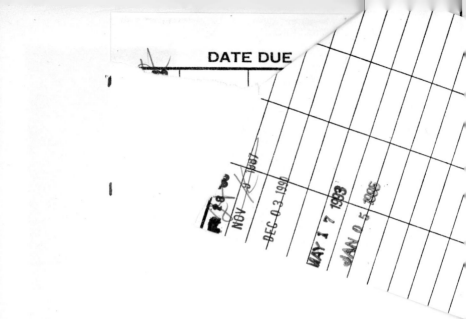